TYCHO PRESS

STOCK MARKET INVESTING

—— FOR ——

BEGINNERS

ESSENTIALS TO START INVESTING SUCCESSFULLY

Copyright © 2013 by Tycho Press, Berkeley, California.

No part of this publication may be reproduced, stored in a retrieval system or transmitted in any form or by any means, electronic, mechanical, photocopying, recording, scanning or otherwise, except as permitted under Sections 107 or 108 of the 1976 United States Copyright Act, without the prior written permission of the Publisher. Requests to the Publisher for permission should be addressed to the Permissions Department, Tycho Press, 918 Parker Street, Suite A-12, Berkeley, CA 94710.

Limit of Liability/Disclaimer of Warranty: The Publisher and the author make no representations or warranties with respect to the accuracy or completeness of the contents of this work and specifically disclaim all warranties, including without limitation warranties of fitness for a particular purpose. No warranty may be created or extended by sales or promotional materials. The advice and strategies contained herein may not be suitable for every situation. This work is sold with the understanding that the publisher is not engaged in rendering medical, legal or other professional advice or services. If professional assistance is required, the services of a competent professional person should be sought. Neither the Publisher nor the author shall be liable for damages arising herefrom. The fact that an individual, organization or website is referred to in this work as a citation and/or potential source of further information does not mean that the author or the Publisher endorses the information the individual, organization or website may provide or recommendations they/it may make. Further, readers should be aware that websites listed in this work may have changed or disappeared between when this work was written and when it is read.

For general information on our other products and services or to obtain technical support, please contact our Customer Care Department within the U.S. at (866) 744-2665, or outside the U.S. at (510) 253-0500.

Tycho Press publishes its books in a variety of electronic and print formats. Some content that appears in print may not be available in electronic books, and vice versa.

TRADEMARKS: Tycho Press and the Tycho Press logo are trademarks or registered trademarks of Callisto Media Inc. and/or its affiliates, in the United States and other countries, and may not be used without written permission. All other trademarks are the property of their respective owners. Tycho Press is not associated with any product or vendor mentioned in this book.

ISBNs: Print 978-1-62315-257-4 | eBook 978-1-62315-302-1

CONTENTS

1

WHY INVEST?

Everybody invests. From the savvy stockbroker on Wall Street to the assembly line worker who skips breakfast every Friday because he runs out of money before his next paycheck, everyone invests their time, effort, and attention in what they find important.

If you spend your Saturdays training for a marathon or tackling 50-mile bike rides, you're investing in your health. If you pack your weekends with family activities, taking the kids to swimming practice or attending Little League games or visiting museums, you're investing in your children. And if you attend classes in hopes that a college degree will help you land a better job, you're investing in your career.

While each of these forms of investing appears to support a different goal, all of them—and dozens more—share a common purpose: to provide for the future. Investing in good health now increases your chances of a happier, more productive retirement. Investing in your family now can build relationships that will sustain in times when you may require more from others yet have less to give in return. Investing in your career now can open professional and financial doors currently out of reach.

Most people reap the richest rewards from their investments after retirement, but the sooner you start planning, the better off you will be in the future. Making even a small commitment to a different kind of investing—the financial strategies presented in this book—can put you well on your way to a longer and stronger retirement.

Common Motivations

Motivations behind financial investing are nearly as numerous as investors themselves. Of course, your priorities may differ from your neighbor's, but for the most part, motivations for investing tend to fall into three categories:

- Investing to build wealth.
- Investing to support a family.
- Investing to prepare for retirement.

Investors focused on building wealth tend to concentrate more on the near future than do other investors. Wealth allows you to establish and maintain a comfortable lifestyle. For some, that comfort might mean a nice-sized house, a couple of reliable cars, and a trip to somewhere warm for a week every January. Many investors are happy with such a lifestyle, while others set loftier goals. By building wealth slowly over time—the safest and surest way to do it—you can improve your lifestyle along with your net worth.

Investors who prioritize supporting a family often seek to accumulate enough wealth now to afford a home in a neighborhood with good schools, the occasional vacation, and things like ballet slippers, algebra tutoring, and summer camp. At the same time, these investors must look ahead to college, which never seems to get any cheaper. All of this is to say that family-oriented investors must be flexible.

Retirement-oriented investors take a longer view than both the wealth builders and the family oriented. You know the type—the type that work hard for 40 years, climbing the corporate ladder. Like most of us, they earn a respectable living without quite reaching the top rungs. Yet they live below their means and always keep one eye on the horizon. The ultimate goal for these investors is a smooth transition to retirement, where even without a paycheck they can maintain the standard of living they spent all those years earning.

Whether you seek to support a robust lifestyle, provide a happy home for your children, or just store enough away so you won't have to work until you turn 80, you can improve the odds of reaching your goals by putting your money to work. Whether you're 20, 40, or 60, you'll enjoy more choices decades from now if you invest wisely—starting today.

And it needs to be today. Not tomorrow, not next week, and certainly not on that mythical day when you suddenly start bringing in more than you spend and can conveniently spare a few hundred a month. People who put off investing until it's convenient spend their golden years eating ramen noodles. You've got to start today.

Not sure how to proceed? Don't panic. By the end of this book, you'll have a clear understanding of your financial goals as well as a number of the tools necessary to reach them. The first step is to avoid making a foolish—but frighteningly common—mistake.

Don't Kid Yourself

Many experienced investors—even some who have amassed millions of dollars in assets—don't really understand what is reasonable to expect from their investments. All too often, they say things like, "I want annual returns of about 20%. But I don't want to take much risk." Statements like these drive money managers to pull out their hair, because they're not a whole lot better informed than saying something like, "I want to eat nothing but bratwurst and pizza for the rest of my life. But I also expect to consume plenty of fiber and few calories in my diet." Greed, bad choices, and stubbornness have torpedoed many an investor, but the biggest hurdle to successful investing might be unreasonable expectations.

Look at Figure 1.1. Over the last 87 years, large-company stocks have averaged annual returns of 11.8%. Over the same period, stocks of small companies delivered a 16.5% average return. Long-term government bonds returned an average of 6.1% a year since 1926, while Treasury bills—about the lowest-risk investment available—managed just 3.6% returns. While both types of stocks handily outperformed bonds, the price of that return was overall higher risk. Small company stocks posted higher highs and lower lows than large companies and bonds, and they were also more likely than large stocks to see returns vary greatly from year to year. Investors call this type of risk volatility. Of course, bond investors didn't suffer nearly as much volatility as stock investors.

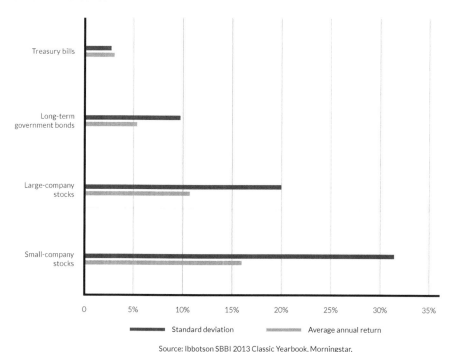

Source: Ibbotson SBBI 2013 Classic Yearbook, Morningstar.

Figure 1.1 - Stocks Outperform Bonds

If you wish to become a successful investor, commit this concept to memory:

"High risk, high return. Low risk, low return."

Like so many important truths, the investment mantra above is simple to understand, but not always easy to implement. Still, the relationship between risk and return is the cornerstone of investing.

Every investment has ups and downs; nothing charts a straight path. However, some paths are rockier than others. The more risk you take, the greater your chance for a high return—or a big loss.

If a stockbroker or financial adviser tells you he can earn high returns with little risk, you've probably found the wrong guy to assist you with your investments.

Set Attainable Goals

Now that you understand the importance of investing and the different types of returns a few of the most common investments generate, it's time to move on to your personal situation. Every individual has different investment requirements and strictures. No investment plan, no matter how shrewd or well considered, applies to everyone. To customize your own financial plan, ask yourself the following questions:

- **What are my goals?** Be specific. "Get rich" won't cut it. Your goals should set specific targets, such as, "Retire with $1 million in assets."
- **How long can I take to reach those goals?** A 40-year-old mother with a daughter who will start college in 10 years must approach investing differently than a 40-year-old with no children who won't touch her investments until she retires at 65.

- **How much risk should I accept?** Some investors can tolerate more risk than others. Some people go cliff diving for relaxation, while others chew their nails at the thought of rain. Neither approach is right or wrong, but you'll sleep better if you tailor your investment approach to your personal feelings about risk.
- **What must I do to meet those goals?** Now you've reached, quite literally, the million-dollar question. Even if you set modest goals, you won't reach them overnight. As Table 1.1 illustrates, the time it takes to feather your nest depends on how quickly your investments grow. Divide 72 by an investment's rate of return, and you know approximately how long it will take to double your money. Earn 4% a year, and your money doubles in 18 years. An 8% return doubles the money in nine years, while earning 12% shortens the doubling time to six years.

Investment growth rate	Number of years to double in value
4%	18
6%	12
8%	9
10%	7
12%	6

Table 1.1

Suppose you have $100,000 in your 401(k) plan and hope to retire in 40 years with $1 million in assets. According to the Rule of 72, if you create a portfolio that returns 6% a year, your account would double to $200,000 by year 12, redouble to $400,000 by year 24, redouble again to $800,000 by year 36, and top $1 million at the end of year 40. Just in time to meet your goal.

Of course, investments never work that neatly. You can't guarantee yourself a 6% return. And sometimes, even if you do manage a 6% annual return, you'll endure a lot of twists and turns along the way—a 30% gain this year, a 15% loss next year, and then a flat year followed by an 8% gain. You get the picture.

Taking the innate uncertainty of investing into account, you should overengineer your investment portfolio. In other words, if you hope to accumulate a certain amount by a certain time, plan as if you need, say, 20% more than your target. Most of all, keep those targets reasonable.

For example, a 30-year-old with no savings and a job paying $40,000 per year who wants to retire a millionaire at age 65 shouldn't require too much risk to reach that goal. A 40-year-old with no savings and a job paying $40,000 per year who wants to retire a millionaire at age 65 will only be able to attain that goal if she is willing to take on some risk. A 50-year-old with two children, no savings, and a job paying $40,000 per year who also wants to pay for his kids' college educations without borrowing and then retire a millionaire at 65, simply does not have a reasonable goal.

At this point you may be asking, "How can I know whether my goal is reasonable?" Figure 1.2 should help.

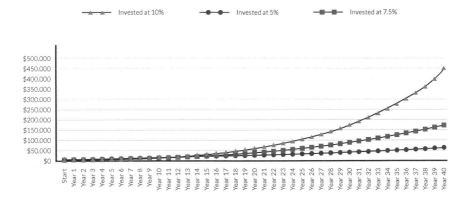

Figure 1.2 - The Power of Time

Too often, investors focus on the gulf between what they have and what they want and become discouraged. Don't fall into that trap, because you haven't embarked on this investment journey alone. You have a powerful ally: time.

Figure 1.2 demonstrates the power of time when it comes to investment. If you can invest at a 7.5% annual rate, $10,000 will grow to more than $20,000 in 10 years, and then to $42,000 in 20 years. After 40 years, that $10,000 will have grown into a $180,000 nest egg.

Investments seem to grow faster in later years because of the effects of compounding. The investment illustrated in Figure 1.2 never actually speeds up its growth on a percentage basis, but as the numbers get larger, the nest egg appears to grow more quickly. For example, suppose you invest $10,000 and earn a 10% return. At the end of the year, you have $11,000. If you duplicate the 10% return in the second year, you'll gain not only another $1,000, but an extra $100—the 10% return on the $1,000 you gained last year. Over time, the excess return earned on past gains will boost your portfolio's value exponentially.

So don't panic. People with 40 years to invest enjoy lots of choices. And while investors with shorter time horizons may have fewer choices, this book can help you make the best choices possible.

2

FUNDAMENTALS OF THE STOCK MARKET

Owners of companies have been raising capital via the sale of equity interests for several thousand years. But the sale of equity interests via a public market dates back closer to 400 years.

Back in the early 1600s, a Dutch shipping company sold shares of itself to raise the capital it needed to expand the business operations. Other companies began offering portions of themselves for sale, and creative entrepreneurs began trading commodities, stocks, and other financial instruments in private markets. A stock exchange opened in Amsterdam in 1611 in response to the increase in the trading of commodities and financial securities. Over the next few centuries, other markets opened throughout Europe.

In 1792, stockbrokers gathered under a buttonwood tree on Wall Street to create a set of rules for buying and selling stocks and bonds—the precursor to the New York Stock Exchange. Today, stocks trade in the United States primarily on three exchanges—the New York Stock Exchange (NYSE), the National Association of Securities Dealers Automated Quotation System (NASDAQ), and the American Stock Exchange (AMEX). Mergers have connected many of the largest exchanges in the United States and overseas. Regional markets also abound, in addition to specialized exchanges that deal in commodities futures, options, and other derivative securities.

The following bullet points will tell you just enough about the most important exchanges so everyone won't assume you're visiting Wall Street for the first time.

- **American Stock Exchange (AMEX)** – For decades the smallest of the three chief U.S. stock exchanges. The American Stock Exchange, often called Amex, sold itself to NYSE Euronext in 2008. While the parent company changed Amex's name to NYSE MKT, the old name has stuck around. This exchange focuses on small-cap stocks, exchange-traded funds, and derivatives.
- **Chicago Board Options Exchange (CBOE)** – The world's largest market for options on stocks, indexes, and interest rates.
- **Chicago Mercantile Exchange (CME)** – The country's largest futures exchange, and the second largest in the world.
- **Nasdaq Stock Market (NASDAQ)** – Commonly called just the Nasdaq, this market is a subsidiary of Nasdaq OMX Group, which operates 24 markets on six continents.
- **New York Stock Exchange (NYSE)** – The oldest, and some say still the most prestigious, stock exchange in the United States. The NYSE is now a subsidiary of NYSE Euronext, a global conglomerate that operates markets that trade more than 8,000 equities and account for nearly 40% of the world's stock trading.

Most large companies and many small ones trade on exchanges to make it easier for investors to purchase their shares. Exchanges require companies to satisfy certain criteria—such as the number of shares available, market cap, share price, and financial benchmarks—before they will list the stock for trading. However, thousands of companies don't list their stocks on exchanges either because they can't satisfy the listing requirements or simply choose not to pay the exchanges' fees. Those stocks trade via networks of securities dealers who negotiate transactions among themselves. Such stocks are said to trade over-the-counter, or OTC.

As OTC stocks tend to be small and less well known than those that trade on exchanges, they have acquired a reputation for risk. Of course, plenty of OTC stocks make fine investments, and many large foreign companies trade over-the-counter. Beginners, however, may wish to steer clear of OTC stocks, particularly penny stocks—stocks that trade at very low prices.

Both the exchanges and OTC markets welcome foreign companies. Firms located outside the United States can register **American depositary receipts** (ADRs) or other specialized securities that allow their stocks to trade on U.S. exchanges. Many U.S. companies take advantage of similar systems to trade on markets in Canada, Europe, or Asia. Never before have investors enjoyed such flexibility to buy and sell securities.

What You Should Know

Once you begin investing, or even researching investments, you'll likely encounter plenty of terms professionals in the field expect you to understand. If you read the *Wall Street Journal* or watch CNBC, journalists will often toss around phrases like "bull market" and "penny stocks" without defining them. If you don't understand a phrase you encounter in the financial media—or something your broker tells you—ask for an explanation or look the term up. Don't get embarrassed about your lack of knowledge. Ignorance can be hazardous to your wealth, and shrewd investors won't buy anything—or fill out a form, answer a personal question, or make a financial commitment—until they understand the ramifications of their actions.

The exchange names presented above are a good start when it comes to learning the vocabulary of investment, but you should take a minute to visit the Glossary at the end of this book as well. It includes many of the most important financial concepts beginning investors should know.

Reading the Glossary won't make you an expert overnight, but it should give you a better idea of what that CNBC anchorman is talking about.

Q&A – 10 Important Questions

Of course, there is a lot more to investing than memorizing a bunch of terms. For answers to 10 questions that beginning stock investors often ask, read on.

Question #1: *How do I start investing in stocks?*

Answer: Open an investment account with a broker. While a few hundred companies allow you to buy your first share of stock directly from them, most companies trade their shares only on stock exchanges or through dealer networks. A brokerage account will give you access to thousands of stocks, as well as thousands of mutual funds and other investments. Most brokers make the account set-up process easy, particularly if you use the Internet. Visit the broker's website and fill out an account application. After you set up the account and send in your money, you can begin making trades. For tips on how to select the right broker, see Chapter 9.

Question #2: *How much money do I need to start investing in stocks?*

Answer: Not as much as many investors think. In a perfect world, you'll jump into the market with $100,000—enough to purchase a diversified portfolio of stocks all at once. But if you don't live in that perfect world, you must set your sights a bit lower. Even if you can spare only $5,000 or $1,000, you can still invest in stocks. Just don't buy as many.

Of course, limiting yourself to just one company's stock, or a small number of stocks, invites risk. But while you take on some risk when you purchase only one or two stocks, choosing not to invest exposes you to another type of risk—poverty. Chapter 10 explains the risks associated with choosing investments in more detail.

If you've set up an account at a discount broker charging $10 per trade, purchasing $1,000 in stock will cost you 1% of your investment in commissions. That means your stock must return about 1% before you recoup the cost of the investment. As a rule, investors should try to limit their commission costs, preferably keeping them below 0.5% of the portfolio value for the year. As the portfolio grows, your trading commissions should decline as a percentage of the assets (See Table 2.1).

Portfolio size	Cost to build 20-stock portfolio @ $10 per trade	% of portfolio	Cost to build 20-stock portfolio @ $50 per trade	% of portfolio
$50,000	$200	0.40%	$1,000	2.00%
$100,000	$200	0.20%	$1,000	1.00%
$500,000	$200	0.04%	$1,000	0.20%

Table 2.1 – Errors of Commission

But if you have only $1,000 to invest, take the leap and pay the commission. After all, you've got to start somewhere. If you commit to investing, you'll be adding new money to the account over time. Spend a few years watching your stocks increase in value, and after a while the commissions won't take such a big bite out of the whole.

Question #3: *I want to buy Apple, but the stock costs several hundred dollars per share, and I don't have enough money to buy 100 shares. Should I stick to cheaper stocks?*

Answer: This question requires two answers. First, regarding the issue of purchasing 100 shares. A couple of decades ago, buying shares in round lots of 100 mattered. Brokers didn't like dealing with smaller trades, and in many cases they charged lower commissions for round lots. Some full-service brokers still prefer to deal in round lots, but with securities trading electronically and discount brokers charging a fixed rate for most trades, today you can buy 87 shares of Stock A and 42 shares of Stock B, and nobody will give you a hard time.

The financial world has evolved, and dollar-based investing has become popular. Dollar-based investing focuses on the size of the stock position in dollars, not shares. Suppose you have $25,000 to invest and wish to purchase 10 stocks. Consider putting $2,500 in each stock, which equates to 50 shares of a $50 stock, 83 shares of a $30 stock, or 29 shares of an $80 stock. Holding equal dollar amounts of all your stocks not only reduces the risk inherent in lopsided portfolios (if your biggest holding falls, it causes a disproportionate decline in the value of your entire portfolio), but also makes it easier to assess how each of your stocks are performing. If you start out with equal-dollar positions, you can tell at a glance which stocks have risen and which have fallen.

The second answer addresses the issue of cheap stocks. Many investors, particularly those who began buying stocks during the days when everyone purchased shares in round lots, still view a $100 stock as more expensive than a $50 stock. However, professionals value stocks relative to earnings, cash flows, or sales, and so should you.

For example, a stock that trades for $100 per share and earns $10 per share has a price/earnings ratio of 10, while a $50 stock that earns $2.50 per share trades at 20 times earnings—and the $50 stock looks more expensive than the $100 stock.

Whether you purchase 50 shares of the $50 stock or 25 shares of the $100 stock, a 10% rise in the stock's price will have the same effect—boosting your holdings in that stock to $2,750 from $2,500.

Question #4: *Which should I buy, stocks or bonds?*
Answer: For most investors, the smart answer is both. Both stocks and bonds play an important role in a portfolio. While stocks offer superior growth potential during good years (as well as a lot more downside potential during bad years), bonds provide greater income and steadier overall returns (though they can't match stocks for potential upside).

While not all stocks trace the same path, they do tend to move in similar directions. If the S&P 500 Index has returned 15% in a given year, for example, most stocks—even those outside of the index—have probably posted positive returns. Some tread more quickly than others, of course.

Bonds also tend to move in the same direction as other bonds, though different classes within the bond group (such as long-term corporate bonds, Treasury bills, high-yield bonds, etc.) will see their returns diverge.

While both bonds and stocks tend to run in loose packs, a fact investors should exploit to reduce volatility is that those packs don't often run together. So, how much should you put in stocks versus bonds? There's no single right answer that applies to everyone. But you can start with this longtime industry rule of thumb: Subtract your age from 110, and you have a good baseline for stock exposure. The equation suggests a 30-year-old should hold 80% stocks and 20% bonds, while an 80-year-old should hold 30% stocks and 70% bonds. Of course, many other factors beyond age contribute to this decision, as discussed in Chapter 11.

Question #5: *How do I know which stocks to buy?*
Answer: Entire books have been written on this topic, but most stock analysis boils down to a few key themes:
- **Value.** Even the fastest-growing stock isn't worth buying if you must overpay. Beginners in particular shouldn't mess around with pricey hypergrowth stocks. Before you buy, consider the stock's key valuation ratios (price/earnings, price/sales, price/book, and price/operating cash flow).
- **Growth.** Even the cheapest stock isn't worth buying if the company can't increase its profits. Rising sales, profits, and cash flow suggest the company's products sell well enough to increase its penetration of the market.

- **Profitability**. Any company can grow if it spends enough money. Well-run companies can maintain their profit margins while still growing. Investors should target stocks with stable or rising profitability.
- **News**. What kind of headlines does the stock generate? Both good news and bad news can affect a stock's price before any changes trickle down to the income statement or balance sheet.
- **Comfort level**. If a stock will keep you up at night for any reason, don't buy it. This rule applies even if the stock skyrockets or if all of your friends load up on the hot name. No investment, even a profitable one, makes sense for an investor who can't buy into the *idea* as well as the stock.

Question #6: *How do I know when to sell a stock?*

Answer: Entire books have also been written on this topic. Most investors find the sell decision tougher than the buy decision because they only buy stocks they like. Once you purchase a stock you enjoy owning, you may find it difficult to part with the investment.

That said, there is no such thing as a permanent buy. Eventually, every stock outlives its utility in your portfolio. All stocks move up and down over time, but the ugly plunge of bank stocks in late 2008 and 2009—far worse than the decline in the broad market—illustrates the dangers of sticking with stocks when their environment changes substantially (see Figure 2.1).

———— Percentage change since Oct. 1, 2008 S&P Banks Select Industry Index
———— Percentage change since Oct. 1, 2008 S&P 500 Index

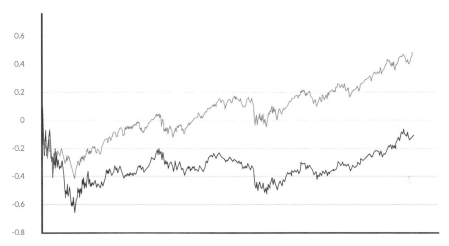

Figure 2.1 - Don't Bank on It

With that reality in mind, consider the following reasons to bail out. When one or more of these statements applies to you or your stock, consider selling it.

1) *The reason you bought the stock no longer applies.* In other words, if you purchased the stock because of its valuation, does the valuation still look attractive? If growth drew you in, has that growth continued? If the answer is no, consider selling.

2) *The company has fundamentally changed.* Sometimes that drug company you purchased because of its pipeline of asthma drugs changes its direction and starts to focus on mental-health treatments. If you like the first approach but not the second, don't be afraid to sell.

3) *The business has fundamentally changed.* Bank stocks illustrate this concept well. Back in late 2007 and early 2008, when a few critics began grousing about banks overextending themselves, many investors bailed out on their stocks. Before that, the rise of

the Internet presaged the decline of newspapers. Investors who heard the train coming and sold their newspaper stocks in 2004 and their bank stocks in 2007 profited from their ability to see and from their willingness to accept the new reality.

4) *You need the money.* This one may sound silly or obvious. But didn't you start investing to build wealth to cover expenses, either now or in the future? If you bought stocks to cope with your daughter's college costs, sell some of them when the first tuition bill comes due, even if you still think all of your stocks make good investments. This does not mean you should sell a few shares just because the car needs new tires. You should have an emergency fund to cover that kind of expense. Even if you purchase stocks with the intention of selling them fairly soon, your stock portfolio as a whole serves a purpose with a longer time horizon.

Question #7: *My stock has declined, but I can't find any news on it. What caused the dip?*

Answer: You may never know. First, you must realize that the stock market reflects the collective will and opinions of millions of investors. If enough of them decide to sell Acme Widget—regardless of their individual reasons—the shares will decline in value.

Sometimes people sell a stock because it has performed well and they wish to book some profits. Stockholders may also sell because shares have begun to fall and they fear additional declines. Sometimes bad news from another company in the industry will cause a stock to decline because the factors driving the weakness in the other stock may affect the first stock. And sometimes stocks sell off in sympathy—perhaps when a close competitor has taken a heavy loss—even when the news doesn't affect them directly; in such cases, they often rebound quickly.

Often a company's stock will move up or down not because of any company-specific news, but because the market itself has taken a turn. Remember that stocks tend to move in a pack. As with any pack, you'll see bold names that bolt to the front while plenty of stragglers hang back. If you own stocks, you should expect them to decline when the larger market declines.

Suppose the broad stock market dips 10% over the course of a couple of months. History suggests that it could still decline further, but eventually most stocks will recover. They always do. If your stock falls 10% in the midst of a widespread market decline of 10% without generating any negative news of its own, you can probably blame the broad market for the decline.

Question #8: *How do I track my portfolio?*

Answer: Twenty years ago, most large newspapers printed daily stock prices, and investors followed their investments in the paper. With the proliferation of websites offering the same information in a more timely fashion, often at no cost, many papers have eschewed the stock pages. These days, the Internet simply offers more information, and a host of financial websites do a fine job of providing pricing and trading data.

You can check out the performance of your stocks on your discount broker's website. While each broker does the job a little differently, they should all show you the value of your stock positions and allow you to view the stocks' history—how they have moved since you purchased them.

If you don't buy all of your investments through the same broker, use a free third-party site to track all of your investments together. Popular financial websites include Yahoo! Finance (www.finance.yahoo.com), Google Finance (www.google.com/finance), and MSN Money (www.money.msn.com). All three of those sites and plenty of others provide free portfolio trackers. Just input your stocks' ticker symbols, and you can create a portfolio of the stocks you own as well as stocks you wish to watch.

Interested in more detail than today's share price? You can also enter the date you purchased the stock as well as the purchase price and the number of shares. If you input your transaction data, the website you selected will show you the returns of each stock since you purchased it—crucial information for assessing your portfolio.

Question #9: *Should I subscribe to a newsletter or go to a broker for help picking stocks? Or am I better off making my own investment decisions and not paying for advice?*

Answer: The answer to this question depends on the answer to two other questions. How much time will you commit to working on your investments? And how comfortable do you feel analyzing numbers?

People who claim to have found the single trick to making money in the stock market shoot e-mails everywhere. "I made 932%, and so can you!" Sometimes they're lying about the return, and sometimes they're telling the truth. Even if an investor did manage to make a 932% return on a stock once, you can't assume he'll do it again. Markets simply don't work that way.

Real stock analysis—the type of research performed by experts who manage other people's money and can get fired if they mess up—takes time. You don't need to commit 40 hours a week, but unless you know you'll spend at least 3 hours a week reading about your companies, following market news, and comparing one stock with another, don't try to go it alone. Find someone you trust—a newsletter editor, a financial planner, or an online guru who actually offers advice without spitting through the computer screen—and pay attention. You don't have to follow anyone's advice exactly, but you'll make better decisions when you can start your own analysis by looking at stocks other people like, or when you can use someone else's strategy to double-check your own selections.

Now, regarding the numbers. More and more, math geeks rule the world. Stock analysis isn't rocket science, and you don't need a PhD in mathematics or statistics to analyze stocks. The job merely requires a flexible mind, a willingness to learn a few new ideas, and a calculator. In Chapters 4 through 7, you'll learn how to analyze stocks from a variety of angles. If you can handle those calculations, you can do your own analysis. (Most high school graduates willing to put in a little effort can handle the math.)

Question #10: *The stock market is falling, but I like the looks of Acme Widget. Should I buy the shares now or wait until the price dips further?*

Answer: Plenty of investors make buy and sell decisions based solely on a stock's price action—a process called technical analysis. Technical analysts look at a stock's price chart and draw conclusions about where it will go based on where it has been. Some people make money this way, and some lose it. However, even experts will agree that predicting and timing short-term stock or market movements is extremely difficult.

This book provides you with the tools to analyze stocks from a fundamental standpoint: by looking at their operating statistics or valuation ratios. Once you identify a stock with strong investment potential at its current price, you take a risk by not purchasing it immediately. Sure, the stock could dip, offering you a chance to snap it up at a bargain. However, the price could also rise, eating away some of your potential profit. As a practical matter, investors who loved a stock at $50 per share tend to find it far more difficult to pull the trigger on the buy after it jumps to $60, even if it rises on good news and the future still looks bright.

Markets often shift direction erratically, and just because stocks have declined over the last week doesn't mean they'll keep declining any more than it means they'll reverse course completely. In most cases, you just can't tell. Unless you have some personal insight about the direction of the stock or the market in the coming days, don't hold off on your purchase in the hopes of buying at a better price.

Keep in mind that after you buy, the market could always go up or go down. Don't kick yourself for acting too soon if the market declines, and don't pat yourself on the back because you bought right before an upturn. If you purchased the right stock, you'll reap your reward in time, regardless of what the market does immediately after you make your buy.

These first two chapters looked at the very basics of the stock market— why to invest, how to get started, and answers to common questions. In the next chapter, we'll take a closer look at the different kinds of investment opportunities that exist today.

3

TYPES OF INVESTMENTS

If you already know about mutual funds, stocks, and bonds, great. But if you think CDs only play music, and the ETF is a government agency, please don't skip this chapter. All five of these popular investment types warrant a place in the average investor's portfolio.

Stocks

Common stocks provide investors with an ownership interest in a company. Shares of stock represent company equity and are often called just that, equities. As discussed in Chapter 2, investors can buy and sell stocks on exchanges—entities that exist mostly to create a marketplace for the shares. Stocks trade constantly during business hours—9:30 a.m. to 4.00 p.m. Eastern time most weekdays—with prices changing from second to second.

As the value of a company rises and falls, so does the value of an investor's stock. Over the long haul, stock prices tend to rise when companies increase their sales and profits. But in the short term, stocks can gyrate, moved by things like overall economic trends, news from rival companies, government action, and a host of other factors.

For example, at the end of August 2013, Microsoft shares sold for $33.40, with about 8.44 billion shares outstanding. If you multiply the number of shares by the per-share price you get $282 billion—the stock's market capitalization, often abbreviated to market cap. An investor who purchases 50 shares of Microsoft for roughly $1,670 would own a tiny fraction of one of the world's largest companies. When more people wish to buy a certain stock than to sell it, prices tend to rise. As any economics textbook will tell you, when products become scarce and the demand for them increases, prices often increase in response. The stock market won't run out of Microsoft shares should they become popular for any reason, but when buyers outnumber sellers, the disparity creates scarcity and drives the price up. The same principle applies on the downside—where an excess of shares and a dearth of buyers leads to falling prices.

Stock-price movements illustrate the importance of the market—the importance of you, the investor—because markets set stock values. The World Bank estimated the value of all U.S. companies' stock at $18.7 trillion at the end of 2012—more than five times the value of companies in each of the next-largest markets, China and Japan. With more than 5,000 U.S. companies trading their stock—not to mention hundreds of foreign companies with stocks that trade in this country—equity investors can tap into just about any facet of the economy.

Not all stocks behave the same way, which means they can play different roles in your portfolio. Here are some classifications every stock investor should understand:

- **Value stocks.** Investors tend to set values for stocks relative to their earnings (or sales, or cash flows, etc). If a stock that earned $100 million over the last year trades at 10 times earnings, its market cap is 10 times $100 million, or $1 billion. In most cases, investors focus on per-share numbers. For example, if the company earning $100 million has 100 million shares outstanding, it earns

$1 per share. A price/earnings ratio of 10 prices the stock at $10 per share. Many academic studies have shown that stocks with low price/earnings ratios relative to the rest of the market tend to outperform. Value-oriented investors gravitate toward value stocks—companies that trade at a discount relative to their earnings or some other operating statistic.

- **Growth stocks.** Stocks with above-market growth of sales or profits tend to outperform their peers. These stocks tend to cost more (higher price/earnings ratios, etc.) than other stocks, as many investors will pay a premium for growth.

At first blush, the idea that both high-growth stocks and value stocks can outperform sounds like a contradiction. But within such a massive system as the stock market, investors have found more than one way to make a profit. You may hear pundits touting the benefits of growth over value, or vice versa. While everyone is entitled to an opinion, this choice mostly comes down to personal preference.

Over the very long haul, value stocks tend to outperform growth stocks. Growth stocks have outperformed value stocks over the last decade, yet value stocks have managed higher returns in 7 of the last 10 years, as shown in Table 3.1. Whether you invest in value stocks, growth stocks, or both, the beauty is that you can make money, regardless of personal preference, if you choose wisely.

Year	Large-company growth stocks	Large-company value stocks
2012	15.4%	23.0%
2011	4.1%	-9.0%
2010	15.9%	21.6%
2009	27.9%	39.2%
2008	-33.7%	-49.0%
2007	14.1%	-6.5%
2006	8.9%	22.6%
2005	2.8%	12.2%
2004	6.5%	18.9%
2003	26.3%	35.0%
Source: Ibbotson SBBI 2013 Classic Yearbook, Morningstar. Data based on the Fama-French growth and value series.		

Table 3.1 - Growth Versus Value

- **Large-capitalization (large-cap) stocks.** The name tells the story. Since investors tend to set values for stocks relative to earnings, companies with massive profits can sport enormous market capitalizations. Stocks of large companies tend to be less volatile, and investors often consider them safer than smaller stocks.
- **Small-cap stocks.** Stocks of smaller companies have historically delivered higher returns than stocks of large companies—again, at the cost of higher risk. What constitutes a small-cap stock? It depends on who you ask, as there is no market consensus on where lies the cutoff point between small and large. A commonly cited dividing line is $3 billion, with anything smaller classified as a small-cap.

Because of their different risk-return profiles, investors should treat large-cap and small-cap stocks as separate asset classes. In general, you should own a blend of large-cap and small-cap stocks in the equity portion of your portfolio. Sure, you could stuff the portfolio with only large-caps or stick to just small-caps, but you might end up with a lower rate of return (the large-cap option) or higher risk (the small-cap option) than you desire.

- **U.S. stocks.** Because economic trends vary from country to country, at times U.S. stocks will thrive while the rest of the world limps along, and vice versa. As a rule, investors consider U.S. stocks safer than foreign stocks. This belief stems, at least in part, from the size and liquidity of the stock market and that U.S. accounting rules require greater disclosure of financial data than most other countries.

- **Foreign stocks.** Many investors purchase foreign stocks to diversify their portfolios. In Chapter 10, you'll learn more about diversification. For now, just realize that you can reduce portfolio volatility and thus reduce risk by blending assets that don't move in the same direction all the time. In addition, you can sometimes boost returns by purchasing stocks of companies in emerging markets like China and India, where the economies grow far faster than in the United States. Of course, those emerging-market stocks come with—you guessed it—more risk.

Pros:

- **Variety.** With the stocks of more than 5,000 companies trading on U.S. exchanges, investors can buy into almost any business they choose.

- **Flexibility.** Stocks trade all day long, which allows investors to buy and sell at specific levels and attempt to play short-term price moves. (The risky strategy of timing intraday fluctuations is called day trading. Even professionals make plenty of mistakes day trading, and beginners shouldn't mess with it.)

- **High returns.** Stocks tend to outperform bonds and other income-oriented investments.

Cons:

- **Volatility.** Stock prices fluctuate more than bond prices. However, investors must accept that risk if they wish to tap into stocks' potentially excellent returns.

- **Complex analysis.** Stock analysis involves looking at a number of statistics, gauging trends, and estimating future growth rates. It takes time and effort, which might explain, at least in part, the popularity of mutual funds.

- **Vigilance required.** Because stock prices can change so quickly, and because they often respond sharply to news about the company or the market, investors must pay close attention to them.

Bonds

Just as stock investors buy equity in a company, bond investors buy debt. Companies and governments issue bonds, collecting cash—the bond's face value or par value—up front from investors. The issuers agree to make interest payments, usually semiannually, for a set time before paying the money back.

In most cases, the payment remains the same for the life of the bond. For this reason, bonds and other securities that make regular payments are classified as fixed-income. In later chapters, during the discussion about how to craft a portfolio, you'll read about seeking a balance between equities and fixed-income (or stocks and bonds).

Estimates vary regarding the size of the U.S. bond market—which contains debt issued by corporations, the federal government, and municipalities—but most peg the bond market at roughly twice the size of the stock market.

Bonds come in many varieties. Here are a few of the most common:

- **Corporate bonds.** Debt issued by corporations.
- **Treasury bonds.** Debt issued by the U.S. Treasury and backed by the full faith and credit of the federal government. Investors both in the United States and overseas generally consider Treasury bonds free of default risk.
- **Agency bonds.** Debt issued by agencies connected to the federal government. While such bonds don't technically have the backing of the U.S. Treasury, most investors assume they have extremely low risk of default.
- **Municipal bonds.** Debt issued by states, municipalities, or agencies connected to states or municipalities, such as water systems. In most cases, the interest payments from these bonds are not subject to federal income taxes.
- **High-yield bonds.** Also known as junk bonds, any securities with a speculative-grade rating fall into this group. Remember the concept: "High risk, high return. Low risk, low return."
- **Convertible bonds.** Companies can issue bonds that, under certain conditions, convert into stock.
- **Variable-rate bonds.** In some cases, bond issuers make interest payments that fluctuate based on changes in a benchmark interest rate.

When you buy a bond, you make a bet on the creditworthiness of the issuer. If a bond issuer can no longer cover the payments, it may default on the bond, leaving investors in the lurch. The risk of default is known as credit risk.

Credit-rating agencies—Standard & Poor's, Moody's, and Fitch Ratings—assess the creditworthiness of companies and governments that issue bonds and assign them ratings. Those ratings reflect the agencies' opinions on the likelihood that the issuer will default. For example, S&P's ratings range from AAA to D, with everything BBB- and higher classified as investment-grade. The agency considers every bond with a rating of BB+ or lower speculative-grade.

Standard & Poor's issues AAA ratings only for the financially strongest companies. Fewer than 15 countries and only four companies earn AAA ratings from S&P.

Many stocks pay dividends, but over the long haul stock investors generate most of their return from price appreciation—the change in the price of the stock. Bonds don't work that way. Their prices will change, but most investors choose bonds because of their interest payments. Because issuers pay back the bonds at the end of their term, also known as maturity, bond prices tend to revert to the face value of the bond as the maturity date nears. Assuming an investor purchases a bond, collects the interest payments, and then recoups the face value of the bond at maturity, the changes to a bond's price along the way don't mean anything.

Unlike stock prices, which tend to fluctuate based on economic and company news, bonds respond mostly to interest rates or changes in a company's perceived credit risk. If a company reports a strong quarter with higher-than-expected profits, the stock price might rise while the bonds remain steady. But if the company announces it has borrowed a lot of money and credit analysts begin to doubt its ability to satisfy its obligations, the company's bonds could lose value.

Bond prices react to changes in interest rates because their fixed payments look more attractive when interest rates fall and less attractive when rates rise. For example, suppose Acme Widget issues $1 billion in 10-year bonds at 5% during a period when the 10-year Treasury yields 3.5%. Since investors can collect a 3.5% yield without risking default, Acme's 1.5% higher interest rate serves as compensation to investors for absorbing the credit risk. If Treasury yields rise to 4.5%, the appeal of Acme's bonds declines; investors demand more than 0.5% for taking on the credit risk of the corporate bond. As a result, Acme's bonds likely dip in price, possibly to a point where they yield roughly 1.5%

more than Treasury bonds. The reverse would happen if Treasury yields declined—Acme could lower its rates accordingly and still be seen as a risk worth taking.

Long-term bonds tend to react to changes in interest rates more strongly than do short-term bonds. Remember, bond prices tend to revert to par value as they near maturity. A bond that matures in three months won't see its value change much even if interest rates migrate, because in three months the issuer will redeem it for its face value. But a bond that matures in 20 years—and has 40 semiannual coupon payments to make before maturity—will react more violently to changes in interest rates, especially as investors reprice the bond to take into account its yield relative to the market.

Pros:

- **Steady income.** Bonds appeal to investors who seek an income stream from their investments. While many stocks pay dividends, few deliver the yield investors can receive from bonds.

- **Safety.** While bond prices do fluctuate, they don't gyrate with the same regularity as stocks. In general, bonds are considered safer than stocks.

- **Diversification.** Bonds offer substantial diversification benefits when paired with stocks in a portfolio. Because bonds tend to take their cues from interest rates rather than the economy or the stock market, they often move in a different direction than stocks.

Cons:

- **Low returns.** Over long periods of time, bonds tend to underperform stocks.

- **Trading difficulty.** While the bond market is massive, it lacks the transparency of the stock market. Investors can't just check

> on the price of their bonds at the Yahoo! Finance website and make instantaneous trades. Discount brokers don't buy and sell bonds at all, and investors seeking to purchase a bond generally must either go through more expensive brokers or contact the bank that makes the market for that bond.
>
> - **Complex analysis.** Bond analysis hinges on assessing an issuer's creditworthiness, a task few people have the training to do well. Most individual investors get their bond exposure through mutual funds, allowing professional credit analysts to do the legwork.

Mutual Funds

Mutual funds pool the assets of multiple investors, providing buying power that exceeds that of all but the wealthiest individuals.

Suppose you have $10,000 to invest. If you try to spread the money around into 50 stocks, commission costs alone might cripple you. But invest that same $10,000 in a mutual fund that owns 50 stocks, and you've purchased a tiny piece of each of those companies without the expense or hassle of acquiring them individually.

Professional money managers decide when the fund buys and sells, and all of the investors win or lose together. If a mutual fund returns 10% in a year, every investor who owned the fund at the start of that year will see the same 10% return on his investment.

At the end of 2012, investors worldwide had $26.8 trillion invested in mutual funds, with $13.0 trillion of those funds in the hands of U.S. money managers, according to the Investment Company Institute (ICI). Of that $13 trillion invested in U.S. mutual funds, 45% was in stock funds and 26% was in bond funds.

Stock and bond mutual funds come in two flavors:

- **Passively managed funds.** Often called index funds, passively managed funds attempt to match the performance of an index.

Indexes—such as the well-known S&P 500 Index of large-company stocks—are baskets of securities constructed to approximate the investment returns of a slice of the financial markets. Most indexes don't change their component stocks often.

- **Actively managed funds.** Unlike passively managed funds, actively managed funds buy and sell securities in an effort to exceed the return of their benchmark—usually an index or group of indexes.

It's tough to overstate the importance of mutual funds as an investment vehicle. In the United States alone, more than 92 million people own mutual funds, often through retirement plans. Additionally, most 401(k) retirement plans invest workers' assets in mutual funds, so if you participate in a company-sponsored retirement plan, you probably already own funds.

Pros:

- **Professional management.** Most individuals don't know much about analyzing investments because of a lack of interest, a lack of training, or both. When you purchase a mutual fund, you're hiring an expert to manage your money.

- **Choice.** With nearly 9,000 traditional mutual funds on the market, just about any investor can find a fund to address her investment goals.

- **Diversification.** Portfolios containing a variety of stocks or bonds tend to be less volatile than an individual stock or bond. Mutual-fund managers use their buying power to purchase multiple securities, which in most cases provide diversification.

Cons:

- **Costs.** Every mutual fund charges fees. If a broker tells you his fund doesn't charge a fee, hang up the phone immediately because he's lying. Remember that expert you hired when you purchased the mutual fund? He doesn't work for free. In addition, some funds charge fees called loads, collecting extra money to compensate the salesperson or investment company.

- **Complacency.** Mutual-fund investors often assume that since they have a professional managing a diversified basket of stocks, they can sit back and relax. Don't make that mistake.

- **Poor returns.** Last year, only about a third of actively managed mutual funds outperformed their benchmarks. Plenty of academic studies suggest this trend isn't new and that fund fees deserve much of the blame. While the chronic underperformance shouldn't scare you away from mutual funds, it should hammer home the importance of choosing your funds wisely.

Exchange-Traded Funds

According to the ICI, at the end of 2012 investors had about $1.34 trillion parked in exchange-traded funds, often called ETFs. ETF assets equate to barely more than 10% of the value of traditional mutual funds, but these types of investments continue to grow in popularity. ETF assets have more than tripled since 2006, while the number of ETFs on the market rose to 1,239 in 2012, up from 359 at the end of 2006.

ETFs operate much like mutual funds in that they commingle the resources of many investors to purchase a basket of stocks, bonds, or both. However, ETFs differ from traditional mutual funds in a few important ways:

- **Trading on exchanges**. As the name suggests, these funds trade on the same exchanges as stocks. ETF prices change from second to second, just like stock prices.
- **Mostly index funds.** While a few ETF managers actively manage their funds in an attempt to top benchmarks, the bulk of them track indexes.

- **Greater transparency.** Unlike traditional mutual funds—which the SEC requires to disclose their holdings quarterly—ETFs must disclose daily. Of course, since indexes don't change their holdings often, most ETFs don't either.

Pros:

- **Convenient trading.** Unlike the way mutual funds reprice at the end of the day and trade only at that price during the following day, ETF prices rise and fall intraday like stocks.

- **Hedging.** Investors can buy and sell options on ETFs, just as they can on most stocks. Beginning investors should probably avoid options, but the freedom to buy and sell options that ETFs allow has contributed to their popularity.

- **Trading costs.** Many brokers charge more to trade mutual funds than stocks. When investors buy or sell exchange-traded mutual funds, they pay the same commissions charged for stock trades.

Cons:

- **Fund expenses.** Remember that every mutual fund charges fees. However, because ETFs trade like stocks, investors frequently treat them like stocks and forget about those fees. And ETFs rarely draw much attention to the fees they collect.

- **Selection.** Most ETFs track indexes, meaning they're passively managed. While some ETFs use active managers, investors seeking active management will find few options among ETFs.

- **Perceived complexity.** While ETFs look like mutual funds in most respects, many investors shy away from them. A 2010 study by Mintel Comperemedia, a consulting firm, revealed that nearly 60% of investors chose not to purchase ETFs because they didn't understand how they worked.

Certificates of Deposit

Traditional certificates of deposit (CDs) act as enhanced savings accounts. Investors give money to a bank, which then agrees to pay a fixed interest rate—generally for a period of five years or less. While investors can withdraw cash from a savings account at any time, CDs require them to keep the funds at the bank until the maturity date. Because of this limitation, they tend to pay more interest than typical savings accounts.

CDs can't replace any of the other investments mentioned in this chapter. They simply provide you with a means to generate more interest on your cash holdings than you'd get from a bank savings account or a brokerage account.

Pros:

- **Safety.** Like other bank accounts, CDs are insured for up to $250,000 by the Federal Deposit Insurance Corporation (FDIC) in the event the bank fails. Brokerage accounts do not receive FDIC coverage, though the Securities Investor Protection Corporation (SIPC) does provide similar, if less comprehensive, protection.

- **No fluctuation.** Because your funds remain in cash, they won't decline in value.

- **Simplicity.** If you understand savings accounts, you already know a lot about how CDs work.

Cons:

- **Low returns.** While CDs generally offer more interest than bank savings accounts, they'll lag behind all of the other investment classes discussed in this chapter over the long haul.

- **No liquidity.** CDs tie up your cash for a period of time. You can access the money if you need it, but you'll pay an early withdrawal penalty or forfeit some of the interest.

- **Separate accounts.** Most investors purchase stocks, bonds, and mutual funds from institutions other than banks. If you keep your cash in a bank CD, you must keep it at the bank, which means you can't redeploy it to purchase stocks or bonds until you transfer the money to a brokerage account.

Alternative Assets

For the most part, new investors should steer clear of anything other than the securities discussed in the preceding pages. Once you dip your toe into the market, you might hear about other investment options, including the following:

- *Commodity futures.* Nearly 100 commodities trade on markets worldwide. They include natural resources such as oil, metals, and lumber as well as agricultural goods such as corn, soybeans, and cattle. Investors can gain commodity exposure by purchasing stock in companies that deal in those commodities, or they can invest directly via a futures contract. Futures contracts allow investors to buy or sell commodities and other assets for predetermined prices in the future.
- *Options.* These derivatives allow stock or ETF investors to bet on whether shares will rise or fall without buying the shares themselves. Suppose a stock trades for $50 per share. If you believe the shares will rise, you might purchase a call option that gives you the right to purchase the shares at $55. When the stock tops $55, you can either purchase the stock at a discount or sell the call option at a profit. Put options allow similar bets to the downside.
- *Hedge funds.* These entities pool investor money like mutual funds do, but they tend to pursue unusual or esoteric strategies. Hedge funds, lightly regulated and often secretive, frequently take on massive risks.

- **Precious metals.** Investors purchase precious metals as a hedge against inflation, or as a backstop to protect wealth against a catastrophe, assuming that when disaster wracks the financial markets, metals such as gold will retain their value.
- **Collectibles.** While investors can make money in collectibles, most lack the market expertise to profit consistently.
- **Real estate.** The only exception to this book's "avoid alternative assets" rule, real estate can diversify a portfolio of stocks, and it acts as a hedge against inflation, tending to rise in value during periods when inflation erodes the price of financial assets. However, if you already own a home, you probably have enough exposure to real estate. Of course, plenty of investors appreciate the inflation protection and total-return potential of real estate and would like to buy in. However, because pieces of real estate cost so much, few individuals have the funds to directly invest in property beyond their personal residences. You can't buy shares of a piece of property on a public market. If you seek real estate exposure, consider real estate investment trusts (REITs). These companies buy, sell, and manage real estate, and their trust units trade on exchanges like stocks.

Weighing the Options

No matter how thoroughly you analyze the options for potential investment, no matter how much care you take in crunching the numbers, no matter how much time you put into studying the stock market and the forces that affect it, you're going to make mistakes. A lot of them.

Don't panic. Nobody gets it right all the time. In fact, excessive boasting about returns and success rates is among the best ways a beginner can spot the posers. Boasters become particularly aggressive during bull markets—when many stocks are hitting new highs.

Legendary investor Warren Buffett once wrote, "Only when the tide goes out do you discover who's been swimming naked." If you listen to the wrong voice, you'll end up high, dry, and possibly embarrassed when the market corrects. And don't kid yourself—it always corrects.

So before you buy into some pundit's foolproof plan, do some of your own work. In the next few chapters, we'll talk about what you can do to better your chances of picking winners—starting with valuation.

4

HOW TO PICK WINNERS, STEP 1

Valuation: Buy Low, Sell High

In theory, every investor wants to buy low. We all understand bargains, and we all prefer buying products on sale rather than at full price. But buying low and selling high isn't as easy as it sounds, because buying low often means diving in while everyone else scrambles to get out of the water. After all, they wouldn't all be leaving unless someone had seen a shark, would they?

The buy low, sell high strategy works better if you focus not on the market, but on a specific stock. If you can determine on your own whether a stock is cheap, you can muster up the fortitude to buy it regardless of the state of the broader market.

Study after study has shown that stocks with low valuations tend to outperform. With those decades of research in mind, here are some valuation ratios to consider:

- Price/earnings ratio.
- Price/sales ratio.
- Price/book ratio.
- Price/operating cash flow ratio.

While investors can calculate dozens of valuation ratios, the four listed above require statistics anyone can gather at no cost, and all four can help you assess a stock's value. The paragraphs that follow and Table 4.1 illustrate all of these ratios for Pfizer, the pharmaceutical titan. To get started, prepare a spreadsheet or printed page similar to the table to keep all the data in one place. You can access all the numbers you need from a free website such as Yahoo! Finance.

Company	Pfizer	Merck	Eli Lilly	Bristol-Myers Squibb
Ticker	PFE	MRK	LLY	BMY
Per-Share Stock Price (End of August 2013)	$28.21	$47.29	$51.40	$41.69
Share Count	7,117	3,010	1,084	1,660
Stock-Market Value	$200,771	$142,343	$55,719	$69,205
Sales, Last 12 Months	$54,427	$44,907	$22,932	$15,806
Per-Share Profits, Last 12 Months	$2.10	$3.47	$3.94	$1.73
Estimated Per-Share Profits, 2013	$2.21	$3.48	$4.12	$1.74
Estimated Per-Share Profits, 2014	$2.31	$3.70	$2.78	$2.01
Operating Cash Flow, Last 12 Months	$16,330	$9,627	$5,163	$6,502
Book Value	$78,511	$47,500	$15,227	$14,371
Price/Earnings Ratio				
Share Price/Per-Share Profits, Last 12 Months	13.4	13.6	13.0	24.1
Forward Price/Earnings Ratio				
Share Price/Estimated 2013 Per-Share Profits	$60,563	$48,356	$23,397	$20,493
Share Price/Estimated 2014 Per-Share Profits	$1.67	$2.61	$3.74	$2.23
Price/Sales Ratio				
Market Value/Sales	3.7	3.2	2.4	4.4

Price/Book Ratio				
Market Value/Book Value	2.6	3.0	3.7	4.8
Price/Operating Cash Flow Ratio				
Market Value/Operating Cash Flow	12.3	14.8	10.8	10.6

Table 4.1 – Valuing the Drug Giants

Price/Earnings Ratio

The price/earnings ratio is the most popular valuation metric, cited often by professionals and amateurs alike. Earnings, or profits, represent what a company has earned after it pays its bills. Valuing a company relative to its profits makes sense. After all, don't you want to generate the maximum profit for every dollar you invest? When you purchase a share of stock, you acquire a tiny piece of a company's earnings. And what the market will pay for those earnings tells you a lot about the company.

To calculate the **price/earnings (P/E) ratio** of a particular stock, you'll need the stock's share price and its earnings over the last four quarters—often called 12-month trailing earnings. Companies report earnings four times a year, with most—including Pfizer—breaking the year down into the three-month periods ending March, June, September, and December. (Some companies report in January, April, July, and October, or February, May, August, and November.)

Visit your preferred financial website, type in the ticker symbol for the stock you wish to analyze, and seek out historical earnings data on the page containing information on earnings estimates. Most pages with estimates will list earnings for the four most recent quarters. Simply sum the earnings per share for those four quarters, and you have trailing 12-month earnings per share. For example, Pfizer traded at $28.21 per share at the end of August 2013, and earned a total of $2.10 per share in the last four quarters, or the 12 months that ended in June. Divide the share price by per-share profits, and you get a P/E ratio of 13.4.

After you calculate the P/E ratio, do the same for other companies in the same industry. You can't just pick other companies randomly, because P/E ratios vary from industry to industry. For example, oil refiners have traded at low P/E ratios for decades. Software companies, on the other hand, tend to command higher P/E ratios than the average stock. If you compare a software company to a refiner, the refiner will almost certainly look cheaper—even if that refiner trades at a far higher P/E ratio than its peers. However, that refiner may not actually represent a better value.

Suppose you select a refiner that trades well above the typical valuation for its industry, and you select a software company that's among the cheapest in its group. Even with a higher absolute P/E ratio, the software company might represent a superior value. Before you make that determination, perform a peer-group valuation comparison and also review the stocks' growth, profitability, and other factors.

In Pfizer's case, comparable stocks include Merck, Eli Lilly, and Bristol-Myers Squibb. Be careful when selecting competitors for comparison. When possible, you want companies that operate in the same markets as your target and which also compete in the same weight class. In other words, if you want to analyze Pfizer relative to other drug companies, select the biggest ones you can find. As the table illustrates, Pfizer trades roughly in line with two of its largest peers—based on P/E—but looks much cheaper than Bristol-Myers Squibb.

While the traditional P/E looks backward, you can also use the ratio to look forward. P/E ratios that use estimates provide another view of the company, one that hints at a story you won't hear from valuation ratios relying on historical numbers. Instead of dividing the share price by earnings over the last 12 months, use the estimate for profits in the current fiscal year or the next year. You can find these estimates at any of the financial websites mentioned earlier.

For instance, Pfizer is expected to grow per-share profits 5% this year and 4% next year. For the most part, analysts don't expect much growth from the big drugmakers. Not surprisingly, since earnings represent the denominator of the P/E ratio, rising earnings will equate to a lower ratio. As of August 2013, Pfizer traded at 12.8 times the profit estimate for 2013 and 12.2 times the 2014 estimate. Pfizer looks somewhat cheaper relative to its peers based on the P/E ratio using the 2014 estimate than it did using trailing profits.

While the P/E ratio effectively gauges value for most companies, it's not perfect. When you consider a company's P/E ratio, keep the following points in mind:

- Earnings do represent the bottom line, but companies can manipulate earnings by changing their accounting.
- Companies that lose money have negative earnings, and valuation ratios mean nothing if the denominator—in this case earnings—is negative. P/E won't work as a valuation tool for unprofitable firms.
- As a rule, industries or companies with higher expected growth tend to sport higher P/E ratios, as the market will pay extra for higher profits in the future.
- When you see a company with an abnormally low P/E, dig a little deeper. The P/E ratio, like all valuation ratios, reflects the company's perceived risk. Suppose a company faces increased competition or new government regulation that could slow its growth. In cases like these, it might deserve a lower P/E. In other words, while some low P/Es indicate bargains, others have become cheap for good reason.

Price/Sales Ratio

The **price/sales (P/S) ratio** focuses on the topmost line of the income statement. Sales, also called revenue, reflect the amount of money a company receives before taking expenses into account. As a raw measure of performance, sales won't tell you as much as profits will. Companies can spend heavily to boost sales, while inefficient operation squeezes little income from that revenue. However, studies show that the P/S ratio is also an effective predictor of future performance. Stocks that are cheap based on P/S ratios tend to outperform more expensive stocks—not unlike the relationship between performance and P/E ratio.

To calculate the P/S ratio, start with the numerator. You can collect sales data on the same website where you grabbed the earnings numbers. Find the link for the income statement and add up the sales for the last four quarters. Multiply the stock's price by the number of shares outstanding—this will give you the stock-market value, or market capitalization. Divide that number by total sales from the last four quarters to derive the P/S. Like P/E ratios, you can then compare the performance of the company in question with others in the industry. For example, Pfizer traded at 3.7 times sales at the end of August 2013—pricier than Merck and Eli Lilly, but cheaper than Bristol-Myers Squibb.

Here are some other issues to consider while analyzing a company's P/S ratio:

- The ratio works for just about every company. While many firms post negative earnings or cash flows, just about all of them have positive sales. When no other ratios work, you can often turn to the P/S ratio for help.
- While sales vary from quarter to quarter and will certainly rise and fall with economic cycles, they don't usually fluctuate as much as other statistics. For that reason, the P/S ratio makes sense for stocks in industries sensitive to cycles, such as companies that sell industrial goods, discretionary consumer products, or semi-conductors. Companies' customers buy more during good times and less when their own situations get dicey. Sales will ebb and flow with that demand, but they generally hold up better than earnings or cash flows.

- Accounting rules for sales offer less leeway than the rules for calculating earnings. As such, the P/S ratio is less susceptible to manipulation by accounting than is the P/E ratio.

Price/Book Ratio

While both the P/E and P/S ratios compare the stock's price to statistics from a company's income statement (also known as the profit and loss statement), the **price/book (P/B) ratio** draws on the balance sheet. While income and cash-flow statements report quarterly numbers that will combine to reflect annual performance, balance sheets simply take a snapshot of the company at a particular time.

To calculate the P/B ratio, divide the stock's market capitalization by the book value, or equity. For example, at the end of August 2013, Pfizer traded at 2.6 times book value—the lowest among the four drug stocks in the table. You'll find the book value on the balance sheet. But instead of summing the equity for the last four quarters, just use the most recent period.

Equity represents assets minus liabilities. In other words, if a company owns $10 billion in assets, and also owes $5 billion, it has $5 billion in equity. Equity—sometimes called shareholders equity or common equity—should reflect the company's liquidation value in theory. If the company goes bankrupt and sells its assets to pay its creditors, it should be left with assets that equal the equity balance.

Of course, because of accounting rules and other factors, book value only estimates liquidation value, and for most companies the estimate would be very rough. The book value of an asset reflects its original cost and may not keep pace with changes in the asset value, either because of inflation, depreciation, or a change in the asset's ability to generate revenue.

That said, the P/B ratio still serves as a useful check of other valuation methods. A stock cheap on P/E and P/S should probably look good based on P/B as well. This won't always occur, but a discrepancy between multiple valuation ratios should raise a flag. In other words, if the stock sports a low P/E but trades at a premium to its peers on P/S and P/B, you'd be wise to learn the reason why before you buy it.

Consider the following when analyzing P/B ratios:

- Only a few companies have negative equity values, which means you can use the ratio with more companies than you can with the P/E ratio.

- P/B works best with traditional businesses that own hard assets—things like factories, machinery, and warehouses full of inventory. Accounting rules also tend to keep equity from fully reflecting the value of intangible assets like patents and other intellectual property. For companies with most of their value tied up in brand names and other intangible assets, book value has little in common with the intrinsic value of the company.

- For companies with extremely heavy debt loads—or ones that have posted serious enough losses to erode the value of equity—the P/B ratio can appear inordinately high.

Price/Operating Cash Flow Ratio

Many investors view **price/operating cash flow (P/OCF) ratio** as the best of the four valuation ratios—and they may have a point.

Remember how companies can skew reported earnings using accounting tricks? Cash flow doesn't leave them many loopholes. To calculate operating cash flow (don't worry, you can pull the final data from the Internet without calculating it yourself), companies start with earnings and then strip away costs that aren't paid in cash as well as other noncash adjustments. Operating cash flow—also called cash from operations—reflects the amount of cash a company's operations generate.

While aggressive accounting methods can skew earnings (and to a lesser extent, sales), and book value becomes less accurate over time, the P/OCF ratio probably offers the cleanest, most accurate picture of a company's valuation. When a company grows earnings but doesn't grow cash flow, investors should become suspicious. If a stock you're considering looks cheap based on the P/E ratio, but expensive on P/OCF, the company might have resorted to accounting shenanigans to boost earnings and make its growth look stronger.

To calculate the P/OCF ratio, divide stock-market value by the operating cash flow generated over the last four quarters. You'll find operating cash flow in the statement of cash flows presented online, again summing the last four quarters. For example, at 12.3 times operating cash flow, Pfizer is cheaper than one of its peers and more expensive than two others.

When you use the P/OCF, remember these points:

- Plenty of companies generate negative cash flows, rendering the ratio useless.
- Many companies don't report cash-flow data—at least not in a way that is accessible to beginning investors. In particular, banks and utilities tend to skimp on providing that kind of information.
- Not all companies calculate cash flow the same way internally. While federal accounting rules provide guidelines, many companies present their own customized numbers in addition to those mandated by the government. When you compare companies using P/OCF, make sure you collect similar numbers for the different companies. Your best option is to pull the data directly from the statement of cash flows—not from the text in a company's earnings release.

Importance of Valuation

Value remains arguably the most popular approach for analyzing stocks, and research suggests it's the most important determinant of stock performance. Stocks with low valuation ratios of all types tend to outperform. However, in the investment world, "tend" is a big word, and by no means implies any kind of certainty.

When studies conclude that stocks with low P/Es tend to deliver higher returns than those with high P/Es, they generally combine data from thousands of stocks and holding periods. When you look at a smaller sample— say, one stock—the trend doesn't always apply. Some stocks with high valuations will perform quite well, and some stocks with low valuations will underperform the market. This often occurs with stocks that trade at a discount to their peers because of weakness somewhere else.

You can't own every stock, and you won't find all the winners. You also can't avoid all the stinkers. You just need to find enough winners to offset your losers, and you can increase your success rate by looking at other attributes besides value.

5

HOW TO PICK WINNERS, STEP 2

Growth: Does Your Company Expand?

Over time, you want your stocks to increase in value. If the market values stocks relative to operating statistics such as sales and earnings, what will it take to drive up the price? Higher sales and earnings. Can stocks appreciate in price without generating growth? For a while, yes. But without growth, eventually those gains will dry up—and sometimes "eventually" means "just about now." You can never be sure when the market will lose patience with a company that no longer grows. For this reason, investors tend to prefer companies that know how to grow.

For example, suppose Acme Widget generated $6 billion in revenue and $1 billion in profit last year. If the stock trades at 2.5 times last year's sales and 15 times earnings, it has a market capitalization of $15 billion. With 1 billion shares outstanding, the shares cost $15 apiece. If Acme posts the same revenue and profit this year and the valuation ratios remain the same, how much will the stock appreciate in value by the end of this year? 0%.

On the other hand, what if Acme invests its cash wisely—in new equipment to broaden its product line, and markets the new goods to its existing customers—boosting sales and profits 20%? Once again, assuming the P/E and P/S ratios don't change, the company's share price will rise to $18, a tidy 20% gain. Of course, these numbers represent an ideal situation. Sales and profits rarely grow at the same rate, and valuation ratios rarely remain steady for long periods of time.

As discussed earlier, companies report operating results on a quarterly basis, and disclose their performance via the media in an earnings release. Investors should read the earnings releases of every stock they own, as well as those of stocks they're considering for purchase. While some companies pack their releases with information and others keep the document sparse, they all present the basics: sales, profits, and share counts.

To view these releases, visit the company's website and seek out the investor relations (IR) section. Some companies make it tough to find their corporate information, but once you locate the IR page, you shouldn't have any trouble downloading the earnings releases and filings with the Securities and Exchange Commission (SEC).

Why mention earnings releases now? Because to assess a company's growth in detail, you'll need to gather some numbers from those releases and SEC filings. Not all growth statistics tell the same story. As a conscientious investor, insist on learning as much of the tale as you can up front. Taken in combination, the following six growth numbers will reveal much about a company:

- Quarterly growth.
- Trailing 12-month growth.
- Four-year annualized growth.
- Estimated current-year growth.
- Estimated next-year growth.
- Estimated five-year annualized growth.

Table 5.1 presents the data you'll need to create your company's growth profile. As with valuation, try to compare the stock's growth to the same numbers for similar companies in the same industry. Remember that stocks with faster growth tend to command higher prices as measured by such valuation ratios as P/E. Start by picking a company, preferably a large, strong one that's been around for a long time. Next step? Read the growth story.

Company	Pfizer	Merck	Eli Lilly	Bristol-Myers Squibb
Ticker	PFE	MRK	LLY	BMY
Last Quarter				
Sales	$12,973	$11,010	$5,930	$4,048
Per-Share Earnings	$0.56	$0.84	$1.16	$0.44
Operating Cash Flow	$3,830	$2,338	$1,637	$1,510
Year-Ago Quarter				
Sales	$13,968	$12,310	$5,601	$4,443
Per-Share Earnings	$0.48	$0.68	$0.83	$0.47
Operating Cash Flow	$4,021	$2,920	$1,306	$1,134
Quarterly Growth				
Sales	-7%	-11%	6%	-9%
Per-Share Earnings	17%	24%	40%	-6%
Operating Cash Flow	-5%	-20%	25%	33%
Trailing 12 Months				
Sales	$54,427	$44,907	$22,932	$15,806
Per-Share Earnings	$2.10	$3.47	$3.94	$1.73
Operating Cash Flow	$16,330	$9,627	$5,163	$6,502

Year-Ago Trailing 12 Months				
Sales	$60,563	$48,356	$23,397	$20,493
Per-Share Earnings	$1.67	$2.61	$3.74	$2.23
Operating Cash Flow	$16,495	$12,884	$6,177	$4,787
12-Month Growth				
Sales	-10%	-7%	-2%	-23%
Per-Share Earnings	26%	33%	5%	-22%
Operating Cash Flow	-1%	-25%	-16%	36%
Last Fiscal Year				
Sales	$58,986	$47,267	$22,603	$17,621
Per-Share Earnings	$2.19	$3.82	$3.39	$1.99
Operating Cash Flow	$17,054	$10,022	$5,305	$6,941
Four Years Ago				
Sales	$48,341	$23,850	$20,378	$20,597
Per-Share Earnings	$2.13	$3.50	$3.88	$1.39
Operating Cash Flow	$18,238	$6,572	$7,296	$3,707
Four-Year Annualized Growth				
Sales	5%	19%	3%	-4%
Per-Share Earnings	1%	2%	-3%	9%
Operating Cash Flow	-2%	11%	-8%	17%
Current Fiscal Year Earnings Estimate	$2.21	$3.48	$4.12	$1.74
Growth	1%	-9%	22%	-13%
Next Fiscal Year Earnings Estimate	$2.31	$3.70	$2.78	$2.01
Growth	4%	6%	-33%	16%
Five-Year Estimated Annualized Growth	5%	3%	1%	8%

Table 5.1 – In Search of Healthy Growth

Collecting Relevant Data

In your company's growth story, consider **quarterly growth** the first sound bite. You can obtain data for the latest quarter—and indeed the last four quarters—from your financial website of choice. Ultimately, the goal here is to calculate year-over-year growth rates, and you won't find the older material in the same place you found more recent numbers. Now it's time to visit the company's website to pull the rest of the data.

Start with the earnings release for the quarter a year before the latest one. Read the release from the top until the company tells you how much it earned in the quarter. Here you must be careful, because the first number you read may not be the one you need. Don't just grab the release for the previous quarter. Comparing June-quarter earnings to March-quarter earnings may be beneficial, but many companies operate seasonal businesses. Year-over-year comparisons (quarter ended June 2013 versus quarter ended June 2012) generally provide greater insight into growth patterns. See "To Everything There Is a Season" for more on the importance of comparing quarters year-to-year.

To Everything There Is a Season

Why is it so important to measure a company's growth relative to the same period a year earlier? Because many businesses see their revenue rise and fall in patterns within the year. If you simply compare the most recent quarter to the one three months ago, you might mess up your growth analysis.

For example, many natural-gas utilities earn a nice profit in the December and March quarters, but routinely lose money in the June and September quarters when the weather is warmer and few customers heat their homes. Additionally, most retailers generate stronger sales during the holiday season than they do for the rest of the year. Per-share profits earned by the department store chain Macy's illustrate this seasonality.

Table 5.2 – Macy's Per-Share Profits for Fiscal Year Ending in January of ...			
Quarter End	2013	2012	2011
January	$2.04	$1.66	$1.57
October	$0.36	$0.32	$0.08
July	$0.67	$0.55	$0.35
April	$0.43	$0.30	$0.10

In each of the last three fiscal years, Macy's earned more in the January quarter than it did in the previous three quarters combined. If you compared Macy's April-quarter results to results from the January quarter, which includes Thanksgiving, Christmas, and the post-holiday period, you'd almost definitely see declining profits. But because of the seasonality of Macy's business, that decline won't tell you much in terms of the overall health of the company and the value of the stock. It is much better to compare the April-quarter numbers to the April quarter of the previous year.

Companies often exclude things from their earnings. For example, a manufacturing company might exclude the money it spent to settle a lawsuit or the gain it made by selling a factory. You might hear these exclusions called unusual items, special items, or extraordinary items. If the company says it excludes these items from its earnings, the analysts who follow the company probably do the same (and so should you). Most companies that exclude items from their earnings will present the adjusted profit number in a table. However, some companies will make you do the calculations. If all this sounds like work, you heard right. Remember, if investing were easy, everyone would do it, and everyone would develop confidence in their stock analysis. But don't worry, the job isn't as tough it sounds—and the actual math is simple.

As long as you've got the earnings release in front of you, grab the quarterly sales numbers as well. Don't worry, you won't have to exclude anything from sales.

Calculating operating cash flow requires some extra steps. For one thing, not all companies present a statement of cash flows in their earnings releases. If yours doesn't, you'll have to dig a little deeper and check out the SEC filings. Just about every company will either provide the filings on their own website or offer links to a third-party site that stores them. To obtain quarterly data, access the Form 10-Q.

After you collect the cash-flow data for the year-ago quarter, you're nearly there. To finish the job, download the earnings release or 10-Q from the quarter immediately before the one you just checked. For instance, if you're looking at the June quarter, pull the March-quarter numbers as well.

While Yahoo! Finance presents cash flow from the four most recent quarters in a quarterly format, most other websites—as well as official statements of cash flows prepared by the companies themselves—present data progressively. In other words, if a company generates $100 million in operating cash flow in the first quarter and $80 million in the second quarter, the second-quarter statement of cash flows will list an operating cash flow of $180 million—the sum of the first two quarters. Unless you start out with the cash flow for the first quarter of a company's fiscal year, you'll need to subtract the value from the previous quarter's statement to obtain a true quarterly number.

Now that you have enough data to calculate the most recent quarter's growth, next up is **trailing 12-month growth**. Essentially, repeat the previous steps—find quarterly earnings, sales, cash flow, and prior year earnings data—until you've collected four quarters, worth of data for each statistic. Sum the quarterly numbers, and you have all you need to calculate trailing 12-month growth.

Now collect the data necessary for calculating **four-year annualized growth**. While calculating four-year growth requires you to go even farther back, annual data requires a lot less work to obtain.

To collect per-share earnings data, download company earnings releases for the fourth quarter of the last fiscal year and for the fourth quarter of the fiscal year from four years earlier. For instance, if the company's last fiscal year ended in 2012, you'll need annual data from fiscal 2008. Find the numbers that exclude all the special items, then record those profits.

Sales and cash flow are even easier. For this stage of the process, visit money.msn.com/investing. Why the MSN site? Because it provides five years of annual data, which neither Yahoo! Finance nor Google Finance does.

Start with the income statement. Choose the option for annual data and grab the sales numbers. After you've gleaned your sales data, move to the cash-flow statement for operating cash flow. Now you've collected all you need for the historical growth rates.

Last, you can find everything you need for the **estimated current-year**, **estimated next-year**, and **estimated five-year annualized** growth rates in one spot.

Visit the analyst estimate page for your stock at Yahoo! Finance or MSN Money and select the following numbers:
- The per-share-profit estimate for the current fiscal year.
- Estimated per-share profits for the next fiscal year.
- Per-share profits for the last fiscal year.
- Growth rate for the next five years.

After you have collected all of these numbers, stop for a minute and pat yourself on the back. You're not done, but the most time-consuming job is behind you. You've already tackled more stock analysis than most investors ever will. Finish doing your research on a few stocks, and you won't be a beginner for long.

Calculating Growth Rates

Now all that remains is the math. Before you begin, review the data for three possible problems.

1) **Negative numbers**. You need two statistics to compute growth rates—the most recent period and the historical period—and your calculation won't mean anything if either of those numbers is negative. You might still be able to draw some conclusions, though. For example, if a company moves from negative earnings or cash flow to positive, that's good news—your stock has gone from a loss to a gain. If a company moves from negative earnings or cash flow to a smaller loss (in other words, from –$1.00 per share to –$0.50 per share), that's often good news as well—your stock has narrowed its loss. Of course, if the loss widens or the stock goes from a profit to a loss, the news has gotten worse.

2) **Blanks**. Perhaps you selected a company that hasn't been around long enough to provide all the needed historical data points. Some companies don't have profit estimates, and if you went with a utility or a financial company, you might not have any cash-flow data. If you can't find any of the numbers needed for a certain calculation, don't try to shoehorn the data you do have into a modified result. Just forget about calculating that growth rate.

3) **Magnitude**. Did you get all the numbers right? If your numbers show a company generating sales of $520 million last year and $48 million the year before, you might want to double-check and make sure you didn't add a zero to last year's sales or leave a number off the previous year's. Sometimes sales really will jump 983%, but not very often. If you actually meant to record $480 million (instead of $48 million) for year-ago sales, the growth rate falls to 9.8%, a far more reasonable number for most companies.

Once you've reviewed all your data, here's how to make the calculations. The examples below feature the numbers for Pfizer presented in Table 5.1, but you can substitute data from your own research.

To calculate growth rate, first divide last quarter's sales by sales from the year-ago quarter, then subtract 1.

Equation

Growth rate = (sales in most recent quarter / sales in same quarter a year ago) − 1

Pfizer example: ($12,973 / $13,968) − 1 = −0.071 = −7%

For Pfizer, that calculation yields a growth rate of negative 7%, meaning that sales fell. Repeat this step for your remaining data from the last quarter as well as the trailing 12 months to come up with trailing 12-month growth.

Annualized growth rates break down long-term growth into one-year chunks. Suppose a stock generated $500 million in sales in 2002 and $740 million in 2012. Those numbers equate to annualized growth of 4% over the 10-year period. If you start with sales of $500 million in 2002 and increase them by 4% each year, by 2012 sales will have grown to $740 million. Of course, operating results don't move in a straight line. Don't assume that a stock with 4% annualized sales growth actually grew its sales by 4% each year. The numbers certainly varied from year to year. However, given sales for two periods more than a year apart, calculating annualized growth rates can give you a sense of a company's overall trajectory.

To calculate, start by dividing sales in the most recent year by sales four years ago. Next, raise that number to the power of 0.25, or one-fourth. Last, subtract one. With Pfizer, this equation reveals an annualized growth rate of 5%.

Equation

> Annualized growth rate = (Sales in last fiscal year / Sales from four years ago) ^ (1 / number of years) − 1
>
> Pfizer example: ($58,986 / $48,341) ^ (1/4) − 1 = 0.051 = 5%

To calculate estimated profit-growth rates for this year and next year, use the equation for quarterly growth above—the one without the exponent—only this time, put profits for the later period as the numerator and profits from the earlier period as the denominator. Since the estimated growth rates only span a single year, you don't need to annualize.

Equation

> Estimated profit growth rate = (Profits for later period / Profits for earlier period) − 1
>
> Pfizer's estimated current-year per-share-profit growth: ($2.21 / $2.19) − 1 = 0.010 = 1%
>
> Pfizer's estimated next-year per-share-profit growth: ($2.31 / $2.21) −1 = 0.044 = 4%

That leaves just one growth number—the five-year profit-growth estimate. This one requires the least work of all; you already collected it from Yahoo! or MSN, and no calculations are necessary.

Comparing Growth Rates

Now that you've gathered your data and computed your growth rates, what should you do with them? Try a three-step process.

1) Compare the growth rates of different statistics for the same period.

For the most recent quarter and for the trailing 12 months, Pfizer managed per-share-profit growth of at least 17%. However, sales and operating cash flow declined during both periods. This disparity suggests that Pfizer's core business isn't growing, yet somehow the company has managed to wring more profit out of its declining base of revenue. What is the most likely cause for such a trend? Gigantic cost cuts that fattened profit margins. And while increasing efficiency is generally a good thing, companies that can't generate growth by bringing in new business or creating new products will often cut deep into their cost structure—sometimes so deep that they further hinder their ability to grow the business.

The four-year annualized growth rates tell a different story, but not necessarily a better one. Pfizer's sales rose by $10 billion over the previous four-year period, managing annualized growth of 5%. But profit growth was sparse, and operating cash flow declined. These numbers suggest Pfizer's struggles with growth didn't just arise in the last year.

Profit estimates suggest Wall Street analysts don't expect much growth from Pfizer, targeting profit expansion of 1% this year and 4% next year. The five-year picture doesn't get much brighter, with the consensus calling for annualized profit growth of 5% over the next five years. That said, modest growth expectations aren't always bad news. The lower the bar, the easier it is for a company to jump over it. While the stock market definitely likes growth, it loves companies that grow faster than expectations.

2) Compare the growth rates of the same statistics over different periods.

Pfizer's per-share earnings have jumped over the last year, but evidence suggests you can't necessarily count on that growth continuing. With annualized growth of 1% over the last four years and expected growth of 5% over the next five, the recent jump looks more like a blip than a trend—a pocket of strength soon to be sewn shut.

Pfizer's sales growth doesn't lend itself to interpretation as clearly as profit growth. The numbers indicate decent growth in recent years, with a major slowdown recently. Such a digression warrants a little extra research if Pfizer makes the cut based on the rest of your analysis.

Operating cash flow tells a cleaner story. It was down slightly over the last four years and down over the last quarter and year. Does anything in those numbers indicate that Pfizer's cash-generating ability should improve going forward? Not really, and this latest conclusion should point you back a few paragraphs to the mention of companies that grow faster than expectations. Pfizer's cash-flow trend doesn't offer much cause for optimism about the company's ability to surprise anyone.

3)Compare the growth rates of the target company with its peers.

Pfizer and all three of the competitors in Table 5.1 saw sales decline over the last year, while two posted lower operating cash flow. These numbers suggest the decline may have something to do with larger forces across the entire drug industry, not just Pfizer. Three of the four drugmakers still managed to grow profits, suggesting other companies have also chosen to cut costs aggressively to compensate for the lack of growth elsewhere.

At the conclusion of the three-step process to analyze its growth, Pfizer doesn't stand out from the crowd, and Pfizer's growth over the last four years doesn't impress. However, most of the other drugmakers also managed feeble or inconsistent growth. Pfizer ranks in the middle of the pack for both growth and estimated growth. Growth-oriented investors might find more to like in the other stocks, though all have glaring weaknesses.

Once you've answered the question of whether or not your company can grow, another query crops up: Does your company know how to grow efficiently?

6

HOW TO PICK WINNERS, STEP 3

Profitability: Making the Most of What You Have

Any company can increase sales if it spends enough money on advertising, marketing, or expansion efforts. But if a firm requires $100 million in expenditures to generate $80 million in new revenue, it may as well not have bothered.

Anyone who has struggled to operate a household on a budget constrained by his income understands the need for profitability. If you can reduce your costs by eating at restaurants less often, switching to a cheaper cable-TV plan, and refinancing your mortgage, you might save enough to pay for that family vacation to Orlando this winter.

While most companies won't cut costs to fund a visit to Disney World, they have other reasons to tighten the belt, and they follow a similar approach as a household. Like individuals on a budget, companies start by identifying unnecessary expenses, then move on to expenditures that may help the company but not enough to actually benefit the bottom line.

For example, what if laying off 70 people or closing that old factory can cut operating expenses to 41% of revenue from last year's 42%?

That half a percent dip in the expense ratio doesn't sound like much, but at the corporate level, where numbers get big, small cuts can mean a lot. For a company with $1 billion in annual revenue, the previous expense reduction would free up $10 million for a marketing campaign, product research, or bolstering the bottom line. Those profits matter, and not only because investors value companies relative to profits. By cutting costs or otherwise boosting efficiency, companies can squeeze more profit *growth* out of their existing resources. Sales not rising fast enough to suit investors? Judicious cost cuts can keep profits growing faster than revenue—at least temporarily.

While improving profitability alone doesn't make a company a good investment, it does suggest both a willingness and an ability to keep expenses under control. Within reason, gains in profitability point to committed, competent management.

Of course you want your companies to at least hold the line on profitability and preferably improve. But moderation is important. Remember the household saving for the Disney trip? What if, instead of cutting back on restaurant visits, the family just slashed its food budget in half? In order to subsist on half of the money, a family that routinely purchased milk and fresh fruit and vegetables might resort to serving nothing but cheap, starchy foods. Sure, costs would go down, but ultimately at the cost of good health. Companies operate in a similar way. Retailers that trim costs by purchasing low-quality goods, drugmakers that skimp on research, or oil companies that stop spending on exploration can become more profitable quickly. Of course, those cuts can also limit the companies' ability to grow revenue and profits going forward.

Gauging Profitability Trends

Even more than growth rates, profitability varies widely from industry to industry. For instance, grocery stores are known for their low profit margins. Like most retailers, grocery stores buy their goods wholesale and mark them up for sale to retail customers. But because of intense competition and consumers' lack of store loyalty, supermarkets must take care when pricing their products. Factor in the costs of operating the stores and paying employees, and most grocers have little margin for error. The five largest U.S. grocery-store stocks average net profit margins of just over 2% of sales. In contrast, software titan Microsoft's net margin tops 25%.

Does this mean investors should buy Microsoft and stay away from Kroger? Not necessarily. Low profitability is a way of life in the grocery business, but that trend is not new, and the market values these stocks accordingly. For a company with a 2% profit margin, a rise to 2.1% can spark impressive profit gains. Just like valuation ratios and growth rates, shrewd investors will consider a company's profitability as it compares to similar companies.

Not only does profitability vary from industry to industry, but it can vary from quarter to quarter as well, exhibiting the seasonality discussed in the section on growth. Once again, department store chain Macy's illustrates the point.

Quarterly Net Profit Margin

Fiscal Year Ending in January of ...

Quarter End	2013	2012	2013	2012
January	7.8%	8.5%	4.8%	4.8%
October	2.4%	2.4%	5.0%	4.5%
July	4.6%	4.1%	5.0%	4.1%
April	2.9%	2.2%	4.9%	3.8%

Table 6.1 - Macy's Trailing 12-Month Net Profit Margin

Macy's generates much higher profit margins during its busiest period—the January quarter. Quarterly margin data shows Macy's increased its net margin in two of the four quarters of its 2013 fiscal year, while the margin eroded during one quarter. The trailing 12-month margin—which considers four quarters of data—explains the trend more clearly. The department store's profitability increased sharply during the fiscal year that ended in January 2012, then hit a plateau in the spring and summer of 2012 before declining at the end of the year.

Of course, changes in profitability from quarter to quarter do have some analytical value, but unless an investor has unlimited time, he should focus his analytical efforts on the most beneficial strategies. For the most part, your profitability analysis should revolve around data for 12-month periods. Investors measure profitability using two sets of ratios:

- **Profit margins** measure profits (often called earnings or income) as a percentage of revenue—another component of the income statement.
- **Returns** on assets, invested capital, and equity compare profits to items on the balance sheet.

You can gather the data you need to assess profitability for most stocks from financial websites and the companies' earnings releases. However, for a few companies that don't provide balance-sheet information in their quarterly releases, you'll need to visit the SEC filings.

Analysis on the Margin

Profit margins measure operating efficiency and show how much of a company's sales it keeps. Taken individually, profit margins may not tell you much. In context, margins and other profitability measures offer plenty of insight.

Margins track a company's efficiency from sales to profits, allowing investors to find weak points. Table 6.2 focuses on three types of profit margins: gross, operating, and net. For this section, the table features Honeywell, a defense contractor.

Company	Honeywell	Lockheed	Raytheon	Northrop Grumman
Ticker	HON	LMT	RTN	NOC
Net Income				
June 2013 Quarter	$1,021	$859	$488	$488
March 2013 Quarter	$966	$761	$490	$489
December 2012 Quarter	$251	$569	$466	$533
September 2012 Quarter	$950	$727	$501	$459
June 2012 Quarter	$902	$781	$472	$480
March 2012 Quarter	$823	$668	$450	$506
December 2011 Quarter	-$310	$698	$539	$550
Trailing 12 Months	$3,188	$2,916	$1,945	$1,969
Sales				
June 2013 Quarter	$9,693	$11,408	$6,115	$6,294
March 2013 Quarter	$9,328	$11,070	$5,879	$6,104
December 2012 Quarter	$9,581	$12,099	$6,439	$6,476
September 2012 Quarter	$9,342	$11,869	$6,045	$6,270
June 2012 Quarter	$9,435	$11,921	$5,992	$6,274
March 2012 Quarter	$9,307	$11,293	$5,938	$6,198
December 2011 Quarter	$9,473	$12,211	$6,422	$6,506
Trailing 12 Months	$37,944	$46,446	$24,478	$25,144
12-Month Net Profit Margin				
Year Ended June 2013	8.4%	6.3%	7.9%	7.8%
Year Ended March 2013	8.1%	6.0%	7.9%	7.8%
Year Ended December 2012	7.8%	5.8%	7.7%	7.8%
Year Ended September 2012	6.3%	6.1%	8.0%	7.9%

12-Month Operating Profit Margin				
Year Ended June 2013	12.8%	9.3%	12.5%	12.4%
Year Ended March 2013	12.5%	9.1%	12.4%	12.3%
Year Ended December 2012	12.2%	8.9%	12.4%	12.4%
Year Ended September 2012	9.8%	8.8%	12.8%	12.3%
12-Month Gross Profit Margin				
Year Ended June 2013	29.1%	11.4%	23.6%	24.0%
Year Ended March 2013	28.8%	11.2%	23.7%	23.9%
Year Ended December 2012	28.5%	11.0%	23.7%	23.9%
Year Ended September 2012	26.3%	10.9%	23.9%	23.4%

Table 6.2 – Gauging Profitability, Part 1

Have you ever wondered why profits are often referred to as "the bottom line?" One glance at an income statement will answer the question. At or near the bottom of the document you'll find a line called "net income" or "net profit." Travel upward from net income and you'll strip out costs, one by one, but you won't find any other costs below net income. It is literally the bottom line.

Net profit margin shows how much of a company's revenue it gets to keep after paying all the bills. To calculate net margin, you'll need data for net income and sales. If the company provides net income excluding special items or discontinued operations, use that number. Otherwise, stick to the true bottom line.

Table 6.2 shows the quarterly net income and sales numbers needed to calculate Honeywell's net margin for the year ending June 2013, and for the years ending March 2013, December 2012, and September 2012. Yahoo! Finance and similar sites provide four quarters of history, so you can tackle the first computation using just the finance site. However, acquiring numbers for the three earlier periods will require a quick stroll through the company's earnings releases.

For the first calculation, sum the net income from the four most recent quarters, and then divide it by the sum of sales from the four most recent quarters.

Equation

> Net margin = Net income / Sales
>
> Honeywell example: $3,188 / $37,944 = 0.084 = 8.4%

To determine Honeywell's net income during the year ended June 2013, sum the results from the June 2013, March 2013, December 2012, and September 2012 quarters. To complete your profitability analysis, you'll work backward one quarter at a time. For example: Net income for the year ended March 2013 consists of data from three of the quarters you already used (March 2013, December 2012, and September 2012), plus June 2012. Remember, always compare income for a given period to sales for the same period.

While all margins present variations on the same theme, each iteration tells a different story. When analyzing net profit margin, keep the following points in mind:

- Lots of companies lose money, and you can't calculate a profit margin when net income is negative.
- If you hear the phrase "profit margin" mentioned without "net" or another word preceding it, the speaker usually refers to net profit margin.
- When net margins change abruptly, be on the lookout for unusual items. Expenditures such as acquisitions and legal settlements frequently skew net income. While most companies will tell you in their earnings releases which items to exclude from per-share

profits, many skip the step with net income. To fix this problem, you can manually adjust your net-income data to account for the excluded items.

Operating profit margin takes into account production and operating expenses, but not taxes or interest payments on debt. It shows us how companies manage expenses beyond the factory. Common expense categories include selling, general & administrative (SG&A)—a combination often referred to as operating expenses; research & development; and noncash costs such as depreciation and amortization.

Most investment professionals consider operating margin the cleanest of the margins and the best for comparing one company to another. Where net income is the bottom line, think of operating income as the middle line. The strength of profit margins as analytical tools lies in their ability to capture profitability at different points along the road from revenue (the top line) to net income.

Most companies' income statements feature a line labeled "operating income" or some variant of the term. That's the number you want. If the company offers you an option for operating income excluding discontinued operations, go with it. You can calculate operating profit margin the same way you tackled net profit margin, just using operating income rather than net income.

Equation

Operating margin = Operating income / Sales

Consider the following when you analyze operating profit margin:

- Companies can exert a lot of control over their operating expenses. As such, changes in the operating profit margin directly reflect choices made by management. Making comparisons between trends in operating margin and trends in net and gross margins can provide hints about the attitude and intentions of company leadership.

- Some companies—though not many—report operating losses. In such cases, rather than try to manipulate the numbers to create a positive value for your margin, just ignore it. For the most part, you won't want to buy companies with operating losses anyway.
- In a few cases, companies will separate depreciation and other noncash costs, stashing them below the operating-income line. For ease of comparison, subtract them from operating income. All of the operating margins in Table 6.2 include noncash expenses.

Gross profit margin takes into account only a company's cost to produce goods. Of course, the concept of production means different things to different companies. Industrial firms might report cost of sales, or cost of goods sold, reflecting the funds spent to cover raw materials, labor, and some manufacturing costs. Other businesses might use terms like "cost of merchandise" or "cost to provide services." The consultant Accenture simply uses "cost of revenue." Fortunately, no matter how a company handles its accounting, you shouldn't have any trouble finding the numbers you need. You should always be able to find a line labeled something like "gross margin" or "gross profit," making data collection on this point easy.

To calculate gross profit margin, just duplicate the steps used for the other types of margin, swapping gross profit for operating or net profit.

Equation

Gross margin = Gross income / Sales

When you review stocks based on gross profit margin, keep these points in mind:

- Accounting requirements leave substantial leeway at this stage of the income statement. Some companies will include more of their operating expenses than others—potentially rendering cross-company comparisons less valid. If you review the numbers of two companies performing the same service—one with a gross margin of 50% and one at 25%—you may find yourself facing an accounting issue rather than a true disparity in efficiency. If this happens, peruse the expense lines between gross profit and operating profit to check for differences in the way the companies account for their costs.
- Unlike operating expenses, production-related expenses tend to be driven by forces outside the company. Possible issues include changes in raw-material costs, issues with a business's supply chain, and increased maintenance expenses for an aging plant. In many cases, management cannot fully mitigate these problems.
- Because of the fungible nature of "production" expenses for companies that don't manufacture products, cross-company comparisons of gross profit margins should carry less weight in your analysis of such companies. However, regardless of how a company calculates gross profit, comparisons versus historical levels can prove useful.
- Some companies—most notably banks like J.P. Morgan Chase—prefer to classify all expenses as operating and don't report any expenses between revenue and SG&A. In such cases, gross profit and revenue will be the same, which equates to a gross profit margin of 100%. You can't draw useful conclusions from numbers like that, so rely on operating and net margins instead.

The trailing 12-month profit margins you've calculated will help you assess a company's profitability trends over the last year, alerting you to recent improvements or regressions in efficiency. However, near-term efficiency trends mean more within a longer context.

You can glean the numbers you need from the income statement at MSN Money, which provides five years of data. No need to revisit the company website or download more earnings releases.

Returning to Profitability

Do you recall the difference between the income statement and the balance sheet? The income statement moves through time—one quarter of net income, followed by another quarter of net income, until you have four quarters. Those four quarters of data combine to paint the operational picture of a year in the life of Honeywell. Balance sheets, on the other hand, don't rely on four quarters of data to make up a whole year. Balance sheets record assets, liabilities, and equity—values that change over time but never go away.

Table 6.3 looks at balance-sheet returns in two ways: first, by assessing trends in the last four quarters, and second, by tracking changes that have occurred over the last five years. To perform the second portion of your profitability analysis, you'll need balance-sheet data for the last eight quarters. The first four or five quarters you can obtain via a financial website. But for the oldest quarters, turn to the company's earnings report. And if your company doesn't include a balance sheet in its earnings releases, download the 10-Qs.

Company	Honeywell	Lockheed Martin	Raytheon	Northrop Grumman
Ticker	HON	LMT	RTN	NOC
Net Income				
June 2013 Quarter	$1,021	$859	$488	$488
March 2013 Quarter	$966	$761	$490	$489
December 2012 Quarter	$251	$569	$466	$533
September 2012 Quarter	$950	$727	$501	$459
June 2012 Quarter	$902	$781	$472	$480
March 2012 Quarter	$823	$668	$450	$506
December 2011 Quarter	-$310	$698	$539	$550
Trailing 12-Month Net Income	$3,188	$2,916	$1,945	$1,969
Assets				
June 2013 Quarter	$42,166	$38,947	$26,376	$27,508
March 2013 Quarter	$41,800	$39,580	$26,687	$25,914
December 2012 Quarter	$41,853	$38,657	$26,686	$26,543
September 2012 Quarter	$41,074	$39,321	$25,697	$25,262
June 2012 Quarter	$40,174	$38,386	$25,078	$25,226
March 2012 Quarter	$40,370	$38,340	$25,627	$25,053
December 2011 Quarter	$39,808	$37,908	$25,854	$25,411
September 2011 Quarter	$39,445	$36,187	$24,120	$25,100
Five-Quarter Average Assets	$41,413	$38,978	$26,105	$26,091
Return on Assets				
June 2013	7.7%	7.5%	7.5%	7.5%
March 2013	7.5%	7.3%	7.4%	7.7%
December 2012	7.2%	7.1%	7.3%	7.8%
September 2012	5.9%	7.6%	7.8%	7.9%

Return on Invested Capital				
June 2013	16.4%	40.0%	14.6%	13.9%
March 2013	16.1%	36.8%	14.5%	13.8%
December 2012	15.6%	34.1%	14.2%	13.7%
September 2012	12.9%	34.6%	14.7%	13.6%
Return on Equity				
June 2013	24.3%	275.5%	22.9%	19.7%
March 2013	24.2%	201.9%	22.7%	19.0%
December 2012	24.0%	162.9%	22.1%	18.8%
September 2012	20.2%	153.9%	22.5%	18.5%
Annual Return on Assets				
2012	7.2%	7.2%	7.2%	7.6%
2011	4.8%	7.3%	7.4%	7.3%
2010	5.5%	7.5%	7.5%	6.6%
2009	6.0%	8.8%	8.3%	5.2%
Annual Return on Invested Capital				
2012	15.6%	40.2%	14.6%	14.3%
2011	10.8%	33.0%	14.1%	13.1%
2010	12.7%	29.5%	14.0%	11.8%
2009	15.2%	38.7%	16.2%	9.8%
Annual Return on Equity				
2012	24.6%	527.9%	23.3%	19.9%
2011	17.3%	113.3%	20.8%	17.5%
2010	20.7%	67.5%	18.4%	15.5%
2009	26.9%	86.5%	20.5%	12.8%

Table 6.3 – Gauging Profitability, Part 2

Returns on assets (ROA), returns on invested capital (ROIC), and returns on equity (ROE) are ratios that function much like profit margins for the balance sheet. While profit margins measure how efficiently a company operates by assessing the profit it can distill from revenue in a given period, returns gauge how effectively it squeezes profits out of its existing resources. As is the case with profit margins—operating margins in particular—trends in ROA, ROIC, and ROE serve as a proxy for the quality of company management. Differences between industries notwithstanding, bigger is better with these ratios. In a vacuum, an ROA of 8% beats 7%. Declines in ROA, ROIC, and ROE suggest the company has trouble finding profitable investments. Additionally, ROA, ROIC, and ROE mean nothing if a company has lost money. If you come up with a negative ratio, just ignore it.

Return on assets measures a company's profitability relative to its entire asset base. The higher the return, the more efficiently the company uses its assets to generate profits. At the end of 2012, Honeywell owned $41.9 billion in assets, up 5% from the previous year. For a mature company like Honeywell, investors shouldn't expect much more in terms of asset growth. Honeywell isn't building new factories all over the globe. Instead, it's focused on making the most of its long-term assets—things like property and equipment—and effectively managing current assets like cash, accounts receivable, and inventory.

The size and composition of asset bases varies widely among companies. Businesses that rely heavily on fixed assets like plants and equipment tend to own more assets than technology firms or companies that provide services. Not surprisingly, capital-intensive businesses with higher asset balances tend to generate lower returns on their assets. For example, in 2012, Dow Chemical posted a 1.2% return on assets, while Google managed nearly 13%.

Even within industries, ROA can differ substantially from company to company. Go ahead and do your cross-checks, but don't be surprised if you see wide variances. However, you won't find such disparities in

Table 6.3. The defense contractors don't have much variation. Three of the four stocks posted a return on assets between 7% and 8% in each of the last four 12-month periods.

Acquisitions can also throw the numbers off. If a company purchases another one, its asset value will jump—and, theoretically, so should the company's profits. However, profits don't always change at the same rate as assets (or invested capital or equity) in the event of an acquisition. So if you see a big jump in assets and other balance-sheet statistics without a similarly strong gain in profits, check the news to see if your company has acquired anything big.

To calculate four quarters of ROA, start with the trailing 12-month net income you used for the profit margins. Divide this by the average value of company assets over the last five quarters.

Equation

ROA = Trailing 12-month net income / Average of total assets for the last five quarters

Honeywell example: ($3,188 / $41,413) = 0.077 = 7.7%

The use of a five-quarter average allows the ROA ratio to capture recent changes in the asset base. The average also compensates for cyclicality in such asset categories as cash holdings, inventory, and accounts receivable, which can vary greatly from quarter to quarter. Because equity and invested capital are components of assets, the asset balance will always be larger than the other two. As such, a company's ROA should be smaller than ROIC or ROE.

As you get started with ROA analysis, consider the following:

- Because banks' balance sheets contain massive amounts of assets, their ROAs always look small. Don't equate the low ROA to a lack of investment appeal.

- Don't underestimate the power of a small change. A company with a 2.0% ROA that boosts it to 2.1% managed the same proportional change as one that moved to 21% from 20%.
- While shareholders tend to show more interest in ROIC and ROE than ROA, many companies rely on ROA as a means to track the changing efficiency of their asset use over time.

Return on invested capital—also called return on investment—narrows the focus to assessing how efficiently a company uses the capital it controls. While there is no universally accepted definition of invested capital, the examples in Table 6.3 define invested capital as common equity plus long-term debt plus preferred stock plus minority interests. Most preferred stock is, in effect, publicly traded debt, while minority interests represent third-party ownership of a company's subsidiaries.

Company managers use ROIC to assess the profitability of divisions within the company as well as to assess the benefits of specific projects. Suppose Acme Widget wants to expand its production capacity, and it can do so by either modernizing an existing factory or building a new one. Acme executives might calculate ROIC for each of the possible strategies, and the company would probably pursue whichever project has the potential to generate a higher ROIC. When you use ROIC to evaluate the profitability of a company, you're adopting the same strategy the company itself may use for its own internal investments.

If your eyes glazed over while reading those last two paragraphs, don't sweat it. Some investors enjoy digging into the statistics, and good for them. But not everyone wants to deal with that level of detail. You need not become an accounting expert to perform ROIC analysis. You can get by if you know two things:

1) Invested capital reflects the total amount invested in the company by everyone, from shareholders to bondholders to other firms that own a portion of one of the company's businesses. In effect, invested capital is the amount of skin in the game.

2) You can find all the components of invested capital easily on the balance sheet.

Calculate ROIC by dividing trailing 12-month net income by average invested capital, and calculate invested capital by adding equity, debt, preferred stock, and minority interest.

Equation

ROIC = Trailing 12-month net income / Average of invested capital for the last five quarters

Invested capital = Equity + Debt + Preferred stock + Minority interest

Just as with ROA, start with profits from the last four quarters and the five-quarter average of the balance sheet statistic. You'll find all four of the components of invested capital on the balance sheet if the company reports them, but not all companies do. Look for long-term debt and minority interest among the liabilities in the middle section. If you don't see any lines with those labels or something similar, don't worry. Not all companies have long-term debt or minority interest.

Additionally, most companies don't have preferred stock. If the company you seek to analyze does have preferred stock, you should find it near the bottom of the balance sheet in the stockholders' equity section. If the company breaks out common equity as its own line, then add the balance for common equity to the balance for preferred stock. However, many companies don't provide a separate line for common equity; instead they lump a variety of values—including preferred stock—together as stockholder equity, shareholder equity, or total equity. If your company goes the kitchen-sink route and groups everything together as stockholder equity, just add that bottom number to whatever debt and minority interests amounts you found earlier.

Before you draw any conclusions about an investment based on its ROIC, consider the following:

- While most companies calculate ROA and ROE the same way, you can't assume the same for ROIC. Some versions of ROIC don't consider preferred stock or minority interest, while others use something other than net profit as the numerator. Don't accept a company's calculation of its own ROIC as a number you can compare to the ROIC of its rivals. Calculate your own ROIC for each company.

- Because of massive differences in the asset bases of many companies, ROIC may be the cleanest of the three return statistics to use for company comparisons within a given industry. The concept of profits as a percentage of the company's available funds to invest makes logical sense.

- If you find a large ROIC discrepancy between two companies with similar ROAs, check their long-term debt. If one carries a substantial debt load and the other does not, then you may have an explanation for the difference in ROIC. Don't read too much into such differences. You don't want to overly penalize a company that borrows unless it carries too much debt. How much debt is too much? If interest payments over the last 12 months consumed more than one-third of operating momentum, or if long-term debt exceeds equity, then you may have uncovered a stock that uses too much leverage.

Return on equity is relied on by professional stock analysts more than either ROA or ROIC. Remember from Chapter 4's discussion of price/book ratios that equity (or book value) consists of assets minus liabilities. Theoretically, if you sold a company's assets and repaid its liabilities, you would walk away with cash equal to book value. For that reason, analysts consider book value an estimate of a company's true liquidation value. However, in the context of ROE, it also means something else.

Suppose Acme Widget owns $1 billion in assets. It has financed those assets with $600 million in liabilities, which leaves $400 million in equity. That $400 million represents the book value of common shares outstanding—usually far below their market value—and earnings retained by the company over time.

ROE calculates the return the company earns just on money stockholders have invested. Because equity doesn't reflect debt or physical assets, ROE represents the most direct assessment of profitability from a shareholder's perspective. A company's equity balance reflects its value above and beyond net worth. If a company makes a profit that exceeds the dividends it pays out, that profit adds to retained earnings. As such, consistently profitable companies tend to grow their equity balance over time. To calculate ROE, divide net income by stockholder equity.

Equation

ROE = Trailing 12-month net income / Average equity for the last five quarters

When you assess a company's ROE, keep these points in mind:

- The same weaknesses that afflict the price/book ratio also affect ROE. Some companies carry negative balances for equity, rendering the ROE meaningless. If you encounter a company with negative earnings and negative equity—which would result in a positive ROE—resist the urge to calculate it. The resulting number won't tell you anything.
- If you multiply ROE and the retention ratio—or the percentage of earnings a company does not pay out in dividends—you calculate the company's sustainable growth rate. In other words, if Acme

Widget has an ROE of 20% and pays out half of its earnings in dividends, it boasts a sustainable growth rate of 10%. While that calculation has flaws—among them overestimating the growth of companies that don't pay dividends—ROE remains a versatile ratio for purposes beyond assessing profitability, including as a proxy for growth.

- Because ROE doesn't take into account debt, it may overstate the profitability of companies that use a lot of leverage.

Annual trends in profitability are the final numbers to consider as we finish up the profitability analysis. Table 6.3 calculates four years of annual ROA, ROIC, and ROE for four defense contractors. You'll have no trouble gathering data for calculating these numbers. Just visit the MSN Money site and pull up your company's balance sheet. There you'll find five years of annual data.

Equation

ROA = Net income for most recent fiscal year / Average assets for two most recent fiscal years

The only difference in the annual calculation versus one using quarterly results involves the denominator. For annual ROA, divide the income by the average of the last two full years' asset balances. You can use a similar equation to calculate annual ROIC and ROE—just change the denominator to focus on invested capital or equity.

Profitable Research

None of the preceding profitability ratios presented mean much by themselves. Considered together, they provide a detailed and comprehensive picture of not just your company in question—say, Honeywell—but its position within its industry.

To best interpret the numbers, try this three-step process:

1) Assess your target company's near-term trends.

Honeywell's profit margins have risen in recent quarters. In the 12 months ended June 2013, net profit margin reached 8.4%, up from 6.3% in the year ended September 2012. Operating margin and gross margin followed upward paths as well, with operating margin up to 12.8% from 9.8% and gross margin up to 29.1% from 26.3%. All three margins rose more between the September 2012 and December 2012 periods than they did between the next two periods combined. What does this tell you? While profitability continued to improve, the rate of overall improvement has slowed. A switch to returns finds similar paths for ROA, ROIC, and ROE, with profitability jumping between the September 2012 and December 2012 periods, and then advancing at a steadier rate.

Taken on their own, rising margins and returns send a positive signal. For example, a high and rising ROE ratio suggests a healthy, fast-growing company becoming more efficient over time. But like every other financial ratio, ROE will sometimes lie to you. Suppose Acme Widget's ROE has risen sharply over the last year. While this could simply reflect equity and profits rising even faster—the situation most investors desire—that's not necessarily the case. If Acme lost money last year, and the loss reduced its equity, then the denominator of the ROE ratio would decline, and the ratio itself could rise even if Acme delivered no profit growth.

A similar scenario played out with Lockheed Martin, one of the Honeywell competitors presented in Table 6.3. During 2012, Lockheed's pension liabilities jumped, knocking its equity value down to $39 million in December 2012 from $2.44 billion in September. That decline showed up in the average equity value. In the year ended December

2012, Lockheed's ROE rose to 162.9% from the already high 153.9% in the year ended September 2012. The ROE has continued to rise as the average equity includes additional quarters with tiny equity balances. Lockheed's equity has also somewhat artificially inflated its ROIC.

Has Honeywell fallen prey to a similar trend, with shrinking assets, shrinking invested capital, or shrinking equity skewing its returns? No, it has not. The table shows its assets trending higher, and a quick review of the company's balance sheets would reveal invested capital and equity generally rising over the last two years.

Sometimes you'll end up looking back at the financial statements to clarify a point or two. Good stock pickers understand that even the most carefully prepared statistics don't always tell the whole story. In this case, you shouldn't have to do any extra work. Honeywell didn't fall prey to either of the two key danger signs:

- Extremely high or low margins relative to similar companies, or relative to its own profitability based on other statistics.
- Sharp swings in returns from quarter to quarter. If trailing 12-month ROE jumps to 20% from 10% just three or four quarters ago, you need to know why.

2) Compare short-term trends to long-term trends.

While Honeywell's net profit margin fell in 2010 and 2011, it rebounded to 7.8% in 2012, a level similar to where it was in 2008. Similar patterns played out with operating and gross margins. ROA, ROI, and ROE all moved in a somewhat similar fashion. However, a lot of companies saw their profitability fall during the recession, so consider Honeywell's short-term volatility a yellow light rather than a red light.

On their own, the long-term trends themselves tell us something about the company's profitability over time. But combined with the more recent margins, we can draw a couple inferences about Honeywell:

- In the most recent period, net margin and gross margin rose above levels seen during most of the last five years. ROA and ROIC also rose above levels seen over the last four years.
- The unusually high profitability—coupled with the slowdown in expansion of profit margins and balance-sheet returns over the last two quarters—suggests the company may have trouble widening its margins and returns much further. By themselves, these numbers shouldn't scare you away from Honeywell; plenty of companies bust out from historical ranges. Still, you can't ignore the possibility that profitability is topping out.

3) Compare the profitability of the target company with its peers.

Over the last year, Honeywell has generated higher net, operating, and gross profit margins than any of the competitors in the table. Based on annual numbers over the last five years, Honeywell typically boasts somewhat higher gross and operating margins than the other companies. When it comes to net margin, that is not so much the case.

Honeywell's ROA of 7.7% in the year ended June 2013 topped the 7.5% earned by the other three companies. With all four companies in the same ROA neighborhood, and with Honeywell not managing the top return in the two previous periods, it's tough to label one as more profitable than the others. However, Honeywell's ROIC and ROE exceed those of two of its competitors. Lockheed earns higher returns, but that company's problem with unusually low equity suggests you should ignore those values.

Measurably more profitable than its peers in four of the six statistics (three types of margin and three types of return), Honeywell stands out from the crowd based on this comparison. The numbers reviewed in the three-step analysis process inspire a few conclusions about Honeywell:

- The company has improved its profitability substantially over the last year, suggesting greater operating efficiency.

- Honeywell already operates more profitably than its peers.
- Honeywell suffered sharper declines in profitability during the economic downturn than the other companies. Possible reasons include a more cyclical business mix or a breakdown in operating efficiency. Regardless of the reason, Honeywell has staged a recovery.
- With profitability already high, Honeywell will need to break out above historical levels to keep improving.

7

HOW TO PICK WINNERS, STEP 4

Putting It All Together

Now you know three different ways to assess a stock: valuation, growth, and profitability. No investor should make a buy or sell decision without reviewing a company from all three angles. And make no mistake, the three concepts you just learned are the beginning, not the end. If value intrigues you, go ahead and dive deeper into the topic. You'll discover a host of valuation ratios and many ways to interpret them. The same goes for growth and profitability. You can spend as much or as little time as you want working on your portfolio. Millions of individual investors have become experts simply by putting in the hours, some of which are spent reading books like this one. They've learned by experience and by doing their homework, just as you're doing now. Until you've assembled the statistics and performed the calculations to determine growth rates or profit margins, you cannot truly understand what the rates and margins mean.

Finding New Stock Ideas

So far the research has focused on Pfizer and Honeywell. For your next analysis project, pick whatever stock interests you. With thousands of stocks available, the task may sound daunting, but it doesn't have to be. Consider these four strategies for inspiration:

- Focus on a stock recommended by someone you trust, particularly if you already know the company, and it looks good from several directions.
- Select a company you like, preferably one that uses a business model you understand. Investment guru Peter Lynch has long counseled to invest in what you know. And you know more than you think. If you work in a steel mill or manufacturing plant, you may already possess the expertise needed to pinpoint which portions of the industrial sector have—and will most likely continue to have—traction. Doctors possess insight on health care, while store managers have a good handle on consumer behavior. Your existing base of knowledge already provides you with a leg up on other individuals who haven't shared your experiences.
- Target an industry, not a company. Suppose you're bullish on hotels, but don't have a favorite. Pick 10 stocks and perform a valuation analysis. That first round of analysis should knock a few off the list. With each round, you can narrow the field further.
- Let your preferred approach lead you. If the concept of growth analysis resonates with you, read stories in the newspaper and on the Internet that focus on growth stocks. In reading interviews with growth investors or stories about growth strategies, you'll encounter lists of stocks that might interest you. Stay away from the tiny, risky, low-profile stocks that few analysts follow, at least until you've amassed more experience.

Maintaining Balance

Whatever method you use to select stocks, and whichever form of analysis you like best, don't abandon a balanced approach. Start with your favorite, then move on to the others. Each of the analysis techniques presented earlier shines light on a stock from a different angle, and while all of the approaches provide tangible reasons to either buy a stock or leave it be, the interplay between the strategies provides the broadest perspective and the fullest picture.

For example, an analysis of Pfizer provided few valuable insights about the appeal of the stock relative to its rivals, but that doesn't mean the mission failed. When you analyze a stock, you seek not only reasons to buy it, but also reasons to avoid it. Sometimes the numbers lead to obvious conclusions—Pfizer doesn't offer much growth potential. At other times, the data does little to differentiate a company from its peers—Pfizer's valuation ratios don't stand out. Growth-oriented investors might prefer one of the other drug stocks to Pfizer. However, compared to other groups, the large-cap drugmakers as a whole offer subpar growth and probably won't appeal to investors focusing on companies able to significantly increase sales and profits. While value investors might not dismiss Pfizer out of hand, the company certainly doesn't distinguish itself based on its valuation.

Just as important as the trends themselves is the interplay among the different characteristics. For example, while profitability analysis did help Honeywell differentiate itself from others in the defense group, current profit margins and balance sheet returns inspire questions about whether the company can continue improving its efficiency. As you move toward any buy or ignore decision, remember the following points:

- In a vacuum, you should favor a cheap stock over an expensive one. However, you should also be aware that stocks often decline in price and command low valuations because of glaring weaknesses in other areas.
- You want to see strong growth in sales, profits, and operating cash flow, but some companies overextend themselves financially

to raise cash to fund expansion. A look at profitability trends can help you spot these troublemakers.

- Hosts of stocks offer either high growth or cheap valuations, but few look good from both angles. If you insist on both growth and value, you will limit your pool of investments. However, the stocks that satisfy your criteria are far more likely to leap off the page.

- Improving profitability is generally a good sign, but when companies take it too far, they can cripple their growth potential. Sometimes increases in profit margins and returns on assets, invested capital, or equity reflect genuine profit expansion, but not all the time. By combining profitability and growth analysis, you can identify companies not only increasing their profits, but also growing them efficiently.

- View extremes with caution. Sure, you want cheap stocks or fast growers. But if your stock trades at 10 times earnings while its peers trade at 20 times, don't rush in. Markets often drive stocks to rock-bottom valuations in response to increased risk. If analysts expect your stock to increase its profits at a 20% annual rate while other stocks in its industry grow only half as fast, expect higher-than-average valuation ratios—and make sure you assess profitability to see whether the company is growing wisely.

Pulling the Trigger

No two stocks are the same, and every time you analyze a stock, you'll find something different. Pulling the numbers from the past three chapters to review Coca-Cola, IBM, or Exxon Mobil would have revealed different strengths and weaknesses than those of Pfizer and Honeywell. And if you wait two or three quarters and revisit Pfizer, the numbers might tell a different story than they did in this analysis.

Pfizer's very lack of exceptional characteristics proves the value of the analysis. Many stocks—in fact, most of them—won't separate themselves from the pack if you look beyond the obvious. As an investor hoping to build wealth by purchasing stocks that will rise—hopefully more than the broad market—you don't want these stocks. A lot of companies excel in one or two areas, but few distinguish themselves with broad-based excellence. You want to find those few, because only the truly exceptional stocks are worth your effort.

Now, don't misread this. If you hold off until you find the perfect stock, you'll spend the rest of your life sitting on your money. Every company has a weakness, and most have several. But that's why you perform the analysis. Find the weaknesses and identify the strengths. When you uncover a stock strong in multiple areas with only a couple of minor flaws, you may have a winner. Then again, you may not. That's just how it goes in the stock-picking business.

Do the three-stage analysis explained in Chapters 4 through 6 to narrow the field. Then move on to the last stage of the stock-selection process—researching the company behind the ticker symbol, as explained in Chapter 8. Finally, when you uncover an opportunity too juicy to resist, pounce on it.

Then do it all again. Because sometimes, no matter how much effort you invest in a stock, that stock will still break your heart. But if you own 25 stocks, you can handle a little heartbreak. It only takes a couple big gainers to offset a few losers. And if you own 25 *high-quality* stocks that have satisfied your exhaustive research criteria, you've probably found a few of those big gainers.

8

HOW TO PICK WINNERS, STEP 5

Getting the News: What the Statistics Don't Tell You

By now, you've isolated a few companies with attractive valuations, solid growth, and strong profitability trends. That kind of fundamental stock analysis can eliminate most of the bad apples. Still, before you buy, set the numbers aside and focus more on the words. Specifically, learn about the company behind the ticker symbol in nonmonetary terms. Plenty of companies look good by the numbers, but statistics rarely tell the whole story.

This chapter provides 10 steps to transition you from a careful stock analyst to a wise stock owner. The first five provide tips for making informed stock purchases, while the second five illustrate some ways to keep your portfolio fresh and vibrant after you buy.

Company Analysis: Beyond the Numbers

1) **Keep up with news about your stocks**. Following the financial news can seem daunting. Thousands of stories compete for your attention each day. You can safely ignore most of them, but if you

own 25 stocks, take the time to read the company releases about financial news or new products. Many portfolio trackers allow you to view headlines related to the ticker symbols on your list. See what analysts and journalists have to say, including their views about competing companies. If Acme's biggest rival has just introduced a new widget that renders your company's key product obsolete, you should know about it.

2) **Subscribe to** the *Wall Street Journal*. If you hope to keep up with the financial markets, no other news source will help you more. The *Journal* has value less as a source of company news than as a gateway to the broad market and the forces that drive it. Plus, the paper offers well-written stories on a variety of topics.

3) **Actually read** the *Wall Street Journal*. Of course, this sounds obvious. But no newspaper has ever spent more time on desks or in briefcases without being used than the *Wall Street Journal*. Plenty of people carry the *Journal* around—often for the same reason some people keep works like *The Critique of Pure Reason* or *Anna Karenina* in a prominent place on a living room shelf, despite never having read the books.

4) **Believe half of what you read, and less of what you hear**. If you want to read Internet columnists or watch CNBC, go ahead. They can provide valuable insight. However, you should also realize that many of these commentators have agendas of their own. While most media outlets at least attempt to remain unbiased, some do the job better than others, and the pundits they interview have no compunction for pushing an agenda.

5) **Never, ever, ever, ever act on a stock tip**. At least not without doing your own research. With more than 5,000 stocks on the market, you can't own all the good ones. Just because someone with a loud voice and a million Twitter followers insists that you buy Acme Widget before it triples doesn't mean the stock makes sense for you—or that it will triple.

Following Through: Keeping Up with Your Stocks

Consider politics for a moment. During an election year, you research candidates, assessing their positions and qualifications. In the end, you select the one you believe will best represent your interests. And then, if you operate like most people, you leave the ballot box and don't think much about your choice until the next election comes around. Four years later, if the guy you elected did a good job, you vote for him again. If he messed everything up, you get the chance to replace him with someone who can do better. Sounds a lot like a stock portfolio.

But stocks offer at least one advantage over politicians. If your stocks tank, you can get rid of them without going through the trouble of justifying and then actually achieving an impeachment. Just sell them and find replacements. No majority opinion needed. Unfortunately, as with politics, too many investors don't follow through on or keep up with their investments. Buying the stock doesn't end the process, because investing is less of a job and more of a journey. You purchase a stock, you monitor the stock, and you sell the stock when it no longer makes sense to own it. Along the way, you'll buy and sell other stocks. Each purchase and sale is a destination along the way.

Conscientious investors—the kind who actually take steps to achieve their financial goals rather than simply dream about them—never really take off their investing hats. Managing your portfolio need not be a full-time job. In fact, it shouldn't take nearly that much time. For most people, spending more than 10 hours a week working on investments reflects poor time management. Of course, spending less than an hour a week reflects foolishness, at least for anyone who wishes to do her own research. Following your stocks generally takes less time—and less math—than analyzing them. The following five steps should give you all you need to keep up with your investments—without turning the task into a second job.

6) **Track your portfolio.** The Yahoo!, MSN, and Google finance websites all offer portfolio trackers, as do a host of other sites, including many brokerages. This advice first surfaced in Chapter 3, but it's worth repeating here: Use one of these services to create a portfolio that includes all your stocks, mutual funds, and exchange-traded funds, and visit it at least once a week. If you're prone to panic whenever you see the red of a price decline on the screen, don't visit more often than a couple times a week. Stock prices change, and even the best ones don't rise every day. Your portfolio will see good days and bad. The better you manage it, the higher the percentage of good days.

7) **Investigate problems**. Say you check your portfolio for the first time in a week and see that Acme Widget has declined 5% since the last time you looked at it. If most of your stocks and the broader market have posted similar declines, Acme probably warrants no extra attention. On the other hand, if Acme has fallen despite steady or rising prices for most of the market, you must find out why.

8) **Reassess your stocks frequently**. You don't need to repeat your statistical analysis every week. Even if a company doesn't generate much news regularly, be sure you think about it from time to time. If shares rise or fall more than 10% from the point when you bought them, you might want to repeat your valuation analysis.

9) **Revisit the financials once a quarter**. Every quarter, companies release the next phase of their growth and profitability metrics (discussed in Chapters 5 and 6). Once your company has updated all its numbers, see if those profitability and growth trends have changed. You may have to wait a while if the company doesn't give you everything in the earnings release. In that case, turn to the SEC filings. This shouldn't take long, as you're just adding the most recent quarter to historical data you've already collected.

10) **Don't overreact to the news**. This may be the hardest advice to follow, and it deserves some extra space. Sometimes your company

posts bad quarterly results, and the shares take a dive. Sometimes government regulators enact new rules that will cost your company money. And sometimes the stock simply declines because of weakness regarding its industry or sector. In all three cases, knee-jerk reactions can cause you to make mistakes.

Stocks often rally the day after bad news sparks a sell-off, and selling immediately on bad news can cost you money. Of course, some stocks do keep going down. For the most part, investors shouldn't try to diagnose long-term effects based on initial media reports—at least not enough to warrant a quick sell decision. Plenty of companies see their stocks dip 10% (or even 20%), only to bounce back to new highs in a few weeks or months. Determining whether or not a troubled stock will accomplish this feat may be the toughest task an investor faces. Of course, there is no single formula for doing it right, because no two situations are alike.

When deciding how to react in the wake of bad news, consider the following points:

- Put more weight on news that affects a company's operations. If a rival comes out with a new product that threatens to take market share, look into it. Has your company historically responded well to such crises, coming out with its own new products? What do analysts who follow the stock say about its ability to compete? If you believe a development will substantially slow sales or profit growth, it might be time to sell.
- Don't get worked up over legal battles. The raft of tobacco lawsuits in the early 2000s changed the way the industry did business, as did the regulatory crackdown on banks after the fiscal crisis of 2008 and 2009. The vast majority of consumer lawsuits and antitrust actions don't have that effect. Additionally, remember those special items companies exclude from their earnings? Legal judgments and settlements generally end up in that category.

While headlines can hurt the stock in the near term, the long-term picture probably hasn't changed much.

- The crowd isn't always right, but most of the time, when the crowd zigs, zagging will get you into trouble. The easiest way to make a fortune is to take a stand and make a big bet when the entire market has bet on the other side. Unfortunately, such strategies can cause investors to lose fortunes even more easily.

If everyone sells the first day, you can equate it to sheep running from danger. The same goes for the second day. But if the share price continues to degrade and the news remains bad, ignore the headlines at your peril. By all means, stick with a stock if you see reason for optimism and if you believe the company can fix whatever problem caused the shares to fall. However, if you lack such conviction, don't fear selling, even if you end up getting it wrong. There's no shame in backing out of what looks like a bad investment and switching into something with more potential. You won't always act at the proper time, and sometimes you'll sell when you should have bought. It happens. But what's the best remedy for missing out on a rally in a stock you sold too soon? The rally you enjoy from the stock you just purchased.

9

THE MECHANICS OF BUYING, SELLING, AND OWNING STOCKS

You've done the hard part. Selecting stocks—by far the most important piece of the equity-investing process—requires more time, effort, and thought than any other part of the job. But your responsibilities don't end there. In fact, they didn't even *start* with stock selection.

Think of stock picking as choosing a route on the journey to financial freedom, understanding, of course, that the route will change often to accommodate the detours and weather hazards that are market fluctuations. In Chapter 10, you'll learn how to steer toward your destination via portfolio management, but neither a map nor a final goal means anything if you don't know how to drive the car.

In this chapter, you'll learn how to select a broker, how to buy and sell stocks through that broker, and how to limit your tax liability. Consider it a quick glance through the driver's manual. Keep your focus on the journey. With some patience and tenacity, you'll get where you need to go.

Who Does Your Trading?

Have you ever asked the question, "So how can I find a good broker, and not someone who will jet off to the Cayman Islands on my dime?" The word "broker" doesn't exactly fill people with confidence, and lots of people have entertained that thought, mostly because a few brokers have indeed absconded with investors' funds. Realistically, if you use a traditional brokerage house, you needn't worry about funding a thief's permanent vacation.

The Securities Investor Protection Corporation (SIPC) works to assist investors harmed by crooked brokers, claiming to have returned assets to 99% of investors eligible for protection. However, the SIPC doesn't help you recoup your losses if you buy the wrong stocks and lose your shirt. In other words, if you get scammed or suckered into a lousy investment, that's your problem. But if a broker steals your money or loses it in the process of doing something illegal or unethical, that's the SIPC's problem.

So don't lose sleep over a broker stealing your money. Instead, focus on picking the right stocks, and focus on what kind of broker to use.

- **Discount brokers**. The name says it all. Discount brokers, such as TD Ameritrade, E*Trade, Charles Schwab, or Scottrade, buy and sell stocks on behalf of investors at lower commissions. However, they also provide no direct investment advice. While the four listed above represent some of the best-known discount brokers, dozens of others offer online trading services for less than $10 per transaction. If you prefer to make trades by telephone, expect to pay a higher commission. For most investors who wish to analyze and select their own stocks or act on advice from a third-party expert, such as a newsletter, a discount broker will do the trick.
- **Full-service brokers**. On top of making trades for you, full-service brokers may also offer advice or perform other services. If you

seek stock advice or your financial situation requires specialized assistance, a full-service broker may make sense. However, be prepared to pay a lot more for your trades—in some cases $50 per transaction or more.

To compare brokers, simply visit their websites and prowl around. Processing stock transactions has become a commodity business, meaning just about all the companies do it well. When you research brokers, look for features important to you, such as:

- **Minimum account size.** Many brokers offer discounts for accounts above $25,000 or $100,000, but low rollers don't get special treatment, and all brokers require minimum balances for accounts. If you plan to start small, make sure your broker can accommodate you. Minimum account sizes often differ.
- **Website design.** Each broker site features its own user interface. You'll find some more intuitive than others, and the ones you prefer may not appeal to someone else. When it comes to navigating a broker's website, rely less on advice from others and more on your personal preference.
- **Volume discounts.** If you plan to make a lot of trades (which, as a beginner, you probably shouldn't), some brokers lower their fees for frequent traders.
- **Variety of securities.** All brokers sell stocks and ETFs. If you plan to buy traditional mutual funds, shop around. Some brokers offer a large number of mutual funds available for no transaction fee, but the selection and prices vary greatly from firm to firm.
- **Research services.** Some discount brokers provide access to online tools, stock screeners, and research reports. A few also let customers interact in online communities where investors share ideas.

If you'd rather avoid brokers altogether, you can buy stocks directly from the company that issued them (or directly from the transfer agent the company hires). Dividend reinvestment plans (DRIPs) allow investors to purchase stocks without a broker. However, many of the plans require that you already own at least one share of stock in your own name before you can participate. DRIPs don't charge brokerage commissions, but most of them assess small fees for purchasing and selling shares.

To get that first stock in your own name isn't too difficult. More than 1,000 U.S. companies offer DRIP plans, and about 600 of them allow you to purchase even your first share through the plan. Alternately, when you purchase stock through a broker, it ultimately belongs to you. Because the broker has custody of the shares, they are held in the brokerage firm's name—usually referred to as the street name—for ease of buying, selling, and transferring. Instead of letting the broker use its street name, you can pay to register the shares in your own name and have the physical certificate sent to you. You can then use those shares to join DRIP plans.

Investors like DRIPs because they allow the reinvestment of cash dividends in company shares, even if the payments are smaller than the share price. For example, if your holdings in a stock trading at $50 per share pay a $5 dividend, you can reinvest the dividend and acquire 0.1 shares of the stock. Many DRIPs also allow you to add money to the account in small amounts—in some cases as little as $10 a month. The ability to gradually add funds to multiple stocks over time appeals to investors who don't have much cash but who do plan to set aside money for investment on a regular basis.

DRIPs attract investors who seek to build wealth slowly and who don't plan to trade frequently. However, because most small stocks (and many large ones) don't offer the plans, DRIP investors enjoy fewer choices. Of course, for many investors, 1,000 stocks still sounds like plenty of selection.

How to Trade Your Stocks

For the most part, beginners should simply buy and sell their stocks at the prevailing price.

Before you actually make a transaction online, visit your broker's website and click on the trading link. The site will ask you how many shares you wish to buy, and whether you wish to make a **market order** or a **limit order**.

When you put in a market order to buy 50 shares of Acme Widget, the broker will make the buy at the best available price. If you've analyzed Acme Widget and like the stock at $40 per share, it shouldn't matter much whether you buy at $39 or $41.

Limit orders, on the other hand, are for investors who want to buy or sell only if the share price reaches a specific level. For example, if you consider Acme too expensive at $40 but would buy it at $35, you can submit a limit order with a $35 price, and the broker will buy the shares if they dip to $35 or below. Limit orders provide greater control over the price paid for a stock, but they can keep investors out of a stock as well. If Acme drops to $35.01, then rises to $50, the investor with the $35 limit order will never buy the stock—and never share in the gains.

Investors also use limit orders on the sell side to lock in gains. Suppose Acme trades for $40 per share, but you'd like to sell and book your profits if the price rises to $45. A limit order to sell at $45 will get you out of the stock at a price no lower than $45, as long as the stock rises to the target level before the order expires. Brokers generally charge higher commissions on limit orders than on market orders.

Reading a Stock Quote

When you open up a financial website and type in your ticker, you'll see a page with a bunch of numbers. While each site designs its pages differently, you can count on seeing most of this information:

Ask price: The lowest price a seller is willing to accept for a security. For most large, heavily traded stocks, the bid and ask price will be close together. For thinly traded stocks, the bid-ask spread can get wide.

Bid price: The highest price a buyer is willing to pay for a security. At any given time, brokers deal with millions of buy and sell orders, some of which indicate a specific price to buy or sell.

Current price: This number reflects the most recent transaction price, though free websites usually operate on a delay, so their numbers are slightly outdated.

Day's range: The high and low prices in the current day's trading.

Fifty-two-week range: The high and low prices over the last year.

Volume: The number of shares traded.

Last, note that if you access a quote page after the market closes, you'll see end-of-day numbers. If you visit during trading hours, you'll find intraday numbers.

Some investors prefer to use **stop orders**—orders that turn into market orders after the stock hits a threshold. For example, Acme trades at $40. You're afraid it will fall hard, so you put in a stop order at $35. If the shares dip below $35, the stop order activates and your broker sells the stock at the prevailing price.

Unfortunately, stop orders have limits. If bad news breaks and the stock immediately dips to $30 per share, you'll sell at about that price. A sell limit order won't guarantee you a sale at $35, just that you'll sell the shares at the going rate once the price dips below $35.

Investors who use stop orders also run the risk of buying or selling stocks simply because the market moves. Suppose you set a stop order at 10% below the stock's current price to protect against ugly losses because you fear the company will lose a patent lawsuit that could cost it millions of dollars in sales. What if the market falls 15% and your stock slides with the rest of them? No lawsuit has surfaced, and the reasons you purchased the stock remain intact. Yet the stop order would have sold you out of the stock, which presumably stands a good chance of recovering when the market regains its momentum.

In short, limit orders allow you to get into stocks if they fall or get out of stocks if they rise. Stop orders allow you to get out of stocks if they fall or get into stocks if they rise. Your broker will offer you plenty of trading options beyond market, limit, and stop orders. As you gain experience, feel free to expand your horizons and experiment with new ways to trade. But whatever you do, no matter your trading goals, never forget the single most important trading rule: If you don't understand how the trade works and why it makes sense, don't make the trade.

Come to think of it, that advice applies to most aspects of investing.

Limiting Your Taxes

Only a fool makes investment decisions without considering the tax implications. On the flipside of that coin, only a fool allows tax concerns to become the chief driver of those same decisions. Far too many investors refuse to sell stocks at a profit because they don't want to pay taxes on the gains. But when the situation changes and it no longer makes sense to hold the stock, failing to sell could cost them.

If you bought a stock many years ago and it has amassed huge gains, congratulations. After all, isn't that the reason you bought it in the first place? If you refuse to sell because you don't want to share with Uncle Sam, you risk watching those gains evaporate. Sure, if you wait long enough, you might be able to sell at a loss and pay no taxes at all. But it's still a loss. Who wins in that trade?

Fortunately, dealing with taxes on your investments is more irritating than it is difficult. With that in mind, here are three questions about taxes every investor must be able to answer.

Question: *How much will I pay in taxes when I collect dividends or sell my stock?*

Answer: Because Congress can change tax rates, this question has no permanent answer. But according to tax rates that took effect at the start of 2013:

- Most stock dividends and bond interest payments will be taxed at the taxpayer's ordinary income rate.
- Short-term capital gains (profits on the sale of stock or other securities) will be taxed at the ordinary income rate. If you sell an asset after holding it for one year or less, you owe taxes at the short-term rate.
- Long-term capital gains will be taxed at 0%, 15%, or 20%, depending on the investor's income.
- Fortunately, you can still use capital losses on your investments to offset income. As always, you only accrue tax liability when you sell your shares. If you buy stock for $1,000 and it skyrockets to $10,000 in a year, as long as you hold onto it as stock, you don't owe a dime of taxes on it.

Question: *How can I protect my investments from tax liability?*

Answer: Individual retirement accounts (IRAs) allow investors to defer taxes on investment proceeds. Some salesmen market IRAs as if only special companies can set them up, and then direct investors to companies that charge large fees to manage the accounts. But that's not how IRAs work. You can set up an IRA at any brokerage, and you can invest in stocks, bonds, mutual funds, and most other financial assets within an IRA.

As of 2013, investors under age 50 can contribute a maximum of $5,500 to their IRA; contribution limits have risen over time, and this trend is likely to continue. In most cases, you can deduct contributions to an IRA from this year's taxes. However, if you or a spouse contributes to another retirement plan through a job, you probably can't. And you can only contribute to an IRA if you or your spouse earns taxable income.

Investors can start taking money out of their IRAs at age 59½, and they must begin after they turn 70½. IRA distributions are subject to federal income tax, and if you remove money from an IRA before the age of 59½, you'll owe federal income tax plus an additional 10% penalty.

A special kind of IRA—the Roth IRA—allows investors to grow their money tax-free. However, Roth IRAs require a few extra hurdles. You can't deduct the contributions, and your income and tax-filing status may limit how much you can contribute.

Question: *My job offers a 401(k) retirement plan. Should I sign up for it?*

Answer: Almost certainly yes. As long as the plan provides you with investment options that don't truly stink, the benefits of a 401(k) are too compelling to ignore.

The 401(k) plan allows your employer to deduct a portion of your salary before taxes and invest it—usually in mutual funds—and some employers will match your contribution up to a certain level. For example, the company might match 50% of what you contribute, up to 6% of your income. If you earn $50,000 and contribute 6%, you'll have $3,000 going into your 401(k), and the company will contribute an additional $1,500 (50% of the $3,000). Company matching funds are as close as most people will ever get to free money. If your employer matches, give yourself a raise by contributing at least enough to max out the employer match.

While your contributions, your employer's contributions, and any dividends and gains in the portfolio are not subject to income tax immediately, as with IRAs, you'll pay taxes when you draw on the funds—usually after retirement.

Individuals who participate in a 401(k) or similar plan through their employers can still contribute to a separate IRA, but they probably can't deduct contributions. If you wish to partake of both tax-preferred investment vehicles, stick to the Roth IRA, which doesn't allow deductions for contributions in the first place.

10

THE POWER OF DIVERSIFICATION

U ntil you've unearthed a gem few other people have noticed, until you've found the wheat among the chaff, and until you've taken a bold step toward your financial goals based on your own analysis, you can't possibly understand how it feels to pick a winner. Once you do achieve some success selecting stocks, you'll probably get the itch to dive back in and find a bunch more. This kind of enthusiasm is good, but don't rush it.

Think of stock selection as you do shopping. After all, the stock market behaves much like a supermarket, allowing you to buy pretty much anything you want, but leaving the decision about which items provide the best blend of good eats and tasty prices entirely up to you.

Suppose that a few hours before you reached the supermarket, the grocer received 10,000 cans of soup when he only ordered 1,000. The excess of inventory would mean it's time for a sale. You, the savvy shopper, notice your favorite brand of tomato soup selling for 25% less than the normal price. Sure, you'll take 20 cans, enough to last you awhile. After you stash the soup in your cart, you tour the aisles to find more bargains, but everything else is the normal price. Sometimes markets behave like that, whether they sell stocks or string cheese.

Now what do you do? You left home with a certain amount of grocery money, planning to return with food for the week's meals. Do you just go home with nothing but a few cans of soup? You have options. You could rush back to the soup aisle and load up—20 cans of chicken noodle, 20 more cream of mushroom, 20 bean with bacon, 20 beef barley, so on. After all, your family loves all of these flavors, so haven't you done what you set out to do?

Of course, you wouldn't choose that option because you know how to shop. You know that your family can't survive (or at least won't be terribly happy or healthy) on canned soup alone, and you would remember the bread and eggs. But for some reason, the "load up on the best deal" strategy that makes no sense at the grocery store somehow manages to capture stock investors' imaginations.

Often, your analysis will identify pockets of strength in the market. If Cisco Systems bubbles to the top of your lists, the same factors that make Cisco look good might also direct you toward Microsoft, Apple, International Business Machines, and Google. All of those stocks could have investment appeal and be worth buying at today's prices. But you can't just buy all five of them and then sit back to watch your portfolio grow—at least not if you want to sleep at night. Just like a diet of only soup, a portfolio containing only large technology stocks lacks diversification. Don't fear the concept; diversification is simpler than the word implies. It essentially believes in safety in numbers—but not just any numbers.

For a moment, head back to the pantry, now stuffed with 120 cans of soup. The soup does the job when a chill wind whips through town. But what about when the sun bakes you? You certainly don't want soup, yet you have nothing else. Plus, you should really eat some vegetables and a more balanced diet if you hope to be anything resembling healthy. Just as you want your pantry to equip your family with meals for all types of weather—and diverse enough meals to maintain your health—your portfolio should also be something that is able to see you through good times and bad.

Sometimes, one company will make a big mistake that sends its stock into the toilet while its rivals do just fine. Sometimes technology stocks will lag while health care stocks set the pace. And sometimes most stocks will decline while bonds rise in value. If you invest, you'll likely encounter each of these phenomena. Diversification is a simple thing you can do to provide some protection against all three.

Diversification Strategies

Investors with diversified portfolios often thrive while others fight for their next meal. Check out these three ways to diversify your portfolio.

1) Buy multiple stocks. Owning 25 to 35 stocks provides the best blend of risk and return. Go with too few stocks, and you take the chance of a couple of stinkers spoiling all the fun. Go with too many, and you lose the benefit of selecting individual stocks. Plenty of investors become stock collectors—buying whenever they find a stock they like, holding them for years, and creating their own little index fund along the way.

Why don't all investors just stick with a portfolio of 25 to 35 stocks? It boils down to two main reasons, one more legitimate than the other.

First, many investors think, "I don't have enough money to buy 25 stocks." For the most part, they're wrong. With discount brokers, investors can purchase stock in $1,000 bites, rather than in 100-share lots. The commission costs can get a bit high with small purchases, but true diversification should save you more in the long run than you'll spend on a few $10 commissions. And even if you only have $1,000 to invest, you can diversify. Spend the money on a stock. Then, when you've set aside another $1,000, buy a second stock rather than more shares of the first one.

Second, investors often worry whether they can keep up with the news on 25 stocks. This objection has some merit; it does take time to follow stocks. However, using the tools introduced in Chapter 7, a conscientious investor can keep up pretty well. If you just don't have the time, you can certainly buy fewer than 25 stocks. Just remember that when you limit the size of your portfolio, you sacrifice some of the benefits of diversification.

2) Buy different types of stocks. Standard & Poor's breaks the market down into 10 sectors:

- Consumer discretionary
- Consumer staples
- Energy
- Financials
- Health care
- Industrials
- Materials
- Technology
- Telecommunication services
- Utilities

Most of the sector names require no explanation. Both consumer staples and consumer discretionary include companies that provide goods or services to consumers. Discretionary stocks (which include hotels, automobiles, clothing, and most types of retail) tend to see their results strengthen and weaken based on economic trends. Staples stocks (grocery stores, tobacco, household goods, and beverages) do business in markets that see less variance because of economic forces. The materials sector contains companies that produce such goods as chemicals, steel, and paper. Telecommunications services—by far the smallest group—consists of companies that provide telephone service.

Cyclical groups tend to see their revenue ebb and flow in cycles, and they include consumer discretionary, industrials, materials, and some technology stocks. Noncyclical sectors include consumer staples, most health care stocks, telecommunications, and utilities. The other sectors include a mix of cyclical and noncyclical stocks, plus a few that simply follow their own paths. It's best to take the "cyclical" and "noncyclical" labels as guidelines rather than rules, as you can find both types of stocks in every sector. The stock market provides investors with far more gray area than black or white.

Not every investor needs to own stocks from all 10 sectors. But if your portfolio doesn't feature stocks from at least six of these groups, you probably haven't diversified enough. You should also vary your stocks by size. Remember that large-caps tend to be safer, while small-caps tend to offer greater growth potential. Last, adding foreign stocks can also diversify your portfolio and possibly boost returns as well. Just remember that you may have more trouble keeping up with the news on foreign stocks—particularly those in emerging markets. They're also more likely to surprise you, both on the upside and the downside.

3) Buy different types of investments. Over time, stock prices tend to move with earnings—rising in value as the underlying company grows. On the other hand, bond prices fluctuate mostly based on interest rates. For example, if Acme Widget doubles its sales and profits over five years, the stock price will probably rise quite a bit. However, the price of Acme's bonds shouldn't change much, assuming steady interest rates and creditworthiness.

Investments that move together have highly correlated returns. If two securities have a correlation of 1.00, they move together step for step. A correlation of −1.00 means they trace exactly opposite paths, one rising while the other falls. On the other hand, a correlation of 0 means the movements are unconnected.

	Large-company stocks	Small-company stocks	Long-term corporate bonds	Long-term government bonds	Treasury bills
Large-company stocks	1.00				
Small-company stocks	0.72	1.00			
Long-term corporate bonds	0.29	0.15	1.00		
Long-term government bonds	0.06	-0.10	0.89	1.00	
Treasury bills	0.10	0.05	-0.02	0.03	1.00

Source: Ibbotson SBBI 2013 Classic Yearbook, Morningstar.

Correlation of Annual Returns

Table 10.1 - Correlation of Annual Returns: Investments Don't Move Together

According to Table 10.1, large-company stocks and small-company stocks have a correlation of 0.72, implying somewhat similar movements, though not exactly the same. Small-company stocks provide some diversification for a portfolio of large-company stocks (as do foreign stocks, which aren't included in the table), but not as much as long-term government bonds, which have a 0.06 correlation. The 0.06 correlation implies that the securities march to different beats, which means that relative to large-company stocks, bonds provide greater diversification than small-company stocks or most foreign stocks.

Remember, bonds are less volatile than stocks, but also offer lower returns (see Table 10.2).

Portfolio	Annual return	Standard deviation	Return per unit of risk
100% large-company stocks	11.8%	20.2%	0.58
90% stocks, 10% bonds	11.2%	18.2%	0.62
70% stocks, 30% bonds	10.0%	14.5%	0.69
50% stocks, 50% bonds	8.9%	11.3%	0.79
30% stocks, 70% bonds	7.8%	9.2%	0.85
10% stocks, 90% bonds	6.7%	9.0%	0.74
100% long-term government bonds	6.1%	9.7%	0.63
Source: Ibbotson SBBI 2013 Classic Yearbook, Morningstar.			

Table 10.2 - The Power of Diversification

From 1926 through 2012, large-company stocks averaged annual returns of 11.8%, with a standard deviation of 20.2%, while long-term government bonds averaged returns of 6.1%, with a standard deviation of 9.7%. That means that in roughly two-thirds of the years, stocks delivered returns between 32% and *negative* 8.4%. In contrast, bonds returned between 15.8% and negative 3.6% about two-thirds of the time—a much smaller range of outcomes.

In addition to being different in terms of risk and potential reward, the returns of bonds and stocks often diverge for long periods. That divergence is what makes diversifying your types of investments to include both so attractive. Beginning investors should generally get their bond exposure through mutual funds. But by all means, capture that diversification benefit. As the two tables illustrate, adding bonds to a stock portfolio reduces both returns and risk relative to a stock-only portfolio.

Return per unit of risk increases as you add bonds, topping out at about 70% bonds to 30% stocks. However, most investors should gravitate to a mix heavier in stocks, boosting the returns while keeping risk manageable.

While there is no way to guarantee that your stock portfolio will weather each and every economic storm, you decrease your risk of losing big with a diverse portfolio. With that, we look at some important questions every investor should ask themselves as they work toward building their perfect portfolio.

11

BUILDING YOUR PERFECT PORTFOLIO

Now that you have a sense of the power and importance of diversification, it's time to create your target portfolio. While this book can provide you with a framework, no formula or cookie-cutter approach will churn out the best asset allocation for every investor. To do this right, you'll need to make a few judgment calls. Start by asking yourself the following four questions.

How Much Do You Need?

Investors can make many types of mistakes as they plan for the future. But perhaps the most common—and the most dangerous—is not knowing how much you need.

Is $1 million enough? That depends on when you retire, how long you live, and how much you plan to spend. Check out the following table, which assumes you manage to sock away $1 million by the time you retire, and then invest well enough to earn 5% per year after inflation. The numbers might surprise you.

Portfolio at retirement	$1,000,000	$1,000,000	$1,000,000
Annual living expenses, rising 3% per year with inflation	$120,000	$100,000	$60,000
Year 1	$930,000	$950,000	$990,000
Year 2	$856,500	$897,500	$979,500
Year 3	$779,325	$842,375	$968,475
Year 4	$698,291	$784,494	$956,899
Year 5	$613,206	$723,718	$944,744
Year 6	$523,866	$659,904	$931,981
Year 7	$430,059	$592,900	$918,580
Year 8	$331,562	$522,545	$904,509
Year 9	$228,140	$448,672	$889,734
Year 10	$119,548	$371,105	$874,221
Year 11	$5,525	$289,661	$857,932
Year 12	$0	$204,144	$840,829
Year 13		$114,351	$822,870
Year 14		$20,068	$804,014
Year 15		$0	$784,214
Year 16			$763,425
Year 17			$741,596
Year 18			$718,676
Year 19			$694,610
Year 20			$669,340

Table 11.1 - Living off $1 Million

Somehow $1 million doesn't look like quite as much money after you crunch the numbers. If you plan to amass a $1 million fortune by retirement, and then live on $120,000 a year each year after you retire, you'd better plan to work until you're 75—or die fairly young. Neither choice would appeal to most investors. (For the record, the retiree who can live on $60,000 a year and sustain a 5% investment return after inflation could stretch his $1 million for 36 years.)

When Will You Need the Money?

If you don't intend to touch your investments until retirement, this question has an easy answer. On the other hand, if you need $100,000 for college costs in 10 years, or if you plan to buy a vacation home years before you retire, now is the time to account for it. As a general rule, the shorter the investment period, the less you can depend on stocks, which tend to be volatile.

Between 1926 and 2012, there have been 66 periods of 20 years—1926 through 1946, 1927 through 1947, etc. Neither stocks nor bonds have ever posted a decline during a 20-year period. Large-company stocks lost value in only 4 of the 78 periods of 10 years, while neither corporate nor government bonds ever had a negative return. When it comes to five-year periods, the picture changes drastically. Large-company stocks declined in 12 of the 83 five-year periods, or roughly 14% of the time. Long-term corporate bonds declined in only 3 of the five-year periods, and it hasn't happened in more than 40 years.

If you're looking 20 years out, keeping mostly stocks in the portfolio makes sense. If you're going to need the money in five years or less, you probably need some extra bond exposure.

How Much Can You Invest?

The answer to this question depends largely on two things: how much you make, and how much you spend to live. You have a lot more control over the second than the first. When it comes to this question, you need to really be honest. Who doesn't believe he's worth $100,000 per year? However, most Americans won't sniff that annual salary.

Fortunately, you can build up a nest egg even if you never make $100,000 per year. Don't believe it? The following table shows how quickly you can build an investment portfolio.

	$100 per month	$200 per month	$500 per month	$1,000 per month
Year 1	$1,200	$2,400	$6,000	$12,000
Year 2	$2,496	$4,992	$12,480	$24,960
Year 3	$3,896	$7,791	$19,478	$38,957
Year 4	$5,407	$10,815	$27,037	$54,073
Year 5	$7,040	$14,080	$35,200	$70,399
Year 6	$8,803	$17,606	$44,016	$88,031
Year 7	$10,707	$21,415	$53,537	$107,074
Year 8	$12,764	$25,528	$63,820	$127,640
Year 9	$14,985	$29,970	$74,925	$149,851
Year 10	$17,384	$34,768	$86,919	$173,839
Year 11	$19,975	$39,949	$99,873	$199,746
Year 12	$22,773	$45,545	$113,863	$227,726
Year 13	$25,794	$51,589	$128,972	$257,944
Year 14	$29,058	$58,116	$145,290	$290,579
Year 15	$32,583	$65,165	$162,913	$325,825
Year 16	$36,389	$72,778	$181,946	$363,891
Year 17	$40,500	$81,001	$202,501	$405,003
Year 18	$44,940	$89,881	$224,701	$449,403
Year 19	$49,736	$99,471	$248,678	$497,355
Year 20	$54,914	$109,829	$274,572	$549,144
Year 21	$60,508	$121,015	$302,538	$605,075
Year 22	$66,548	$133,096	$332,741	$665,481
Year 23	$73,072	$146,144	$365,360	$730,720
Year 24	$80,118	$160,235	$400,589	$801,177
Year 25	$87,727	$175,454	$438,636	$877,271
Year 26	$95,945	$191,891	$479,726	$959,453
Year 27	$104,821	$209,642	$524,105	$1,048,209
Year 28	$114,407	$228,813	$572,033	$1,144,066
Year 29	$124,759	$249,518	$623,796	$1,247,591
Year 30	$135,940	$271,880	$679,699	$1,359,399

Table 11.2 - Building Wealth a Month at a Time

These are not bad numbers, and they assume you never get a raise—and thus never increase your monthly investment. Of course, the more you can set aside, the more you'll have when you need it. And herein lies the most important key to building wealth: Spend less than you make.

Regardless of what your investments do from year to year—and you certainly can't count on them delivering such steady growth—if you spend less than you make every single year, you'll earn enough to support yourself and set some aside.

How Much Risk Can You Handle?

Some investors require a 10% annual return to meet their financial objectives. That's a high hurdle. People have managed it, but achieving 10% annual returns over a long period of time would tax both the skill and the luck of most professional investors, let alone that of beginners. What if the kind of securities needed to make a run at 10% annual returns will keep you up at night? Then you have two choices:

1) Live in fear. (This is not ideal.)
2) Alter your objectives so you can meet your goals with a less risky portfolio.

A lot of people choose option one, but option two makes the most sense, both for your portfolio and for your nerves.

In the investment business, fear of uncertainty is called risk aversion. In most cases, the term applies to fear of investment declines or volatility. Everyone fears losing all their money, but that isn't really the issue here. Stocks are very likely to deliver excellent returns over a 20-year period, but you can't just sit in your rocking chair and wait 20 years. Investing in the stock market involves living with the movements of your stocks day-to-day and year-to-year. And that's where risk aversion comes in. Everyone has some level of risk aversion. The higher your level of risk aversion (the greater your fear of loss), the less risk you can tolerate.

Your level of wealth also affects your risk tolerance. If you have $1 million in the bank, earn a nice living, and won't need your investments for 20 years, you can afford to take more risks than someone with $10,000 in the bank.

Running the Numbers

Once you answer the four key questions, you'll better understand what you need from your portfolio. And with that knowledge comes power.

Questions one and two—how much money do you need, and when do you need it—will help you determine your required rate of return. The following equation will give you a rate of return for any starting and ending point, assuming you wish to grow a basket of money and do not plan to add any new funds:

(What you need / What you have) ^ (1 / Years until you need it) − 1

For example, if you need $1 million, and you have $100,000, and you plan to retire in 25 years, it looks like this:

($1,000,000 / $100,000) ^ (1 / 25) − 1 = 0.096 = 9.6%

But what if you have nothing, yet you can commit funds to invest over time? You can easily create a table like the wealth-building one earlier to plot different scenarios. Here's the equation:

[Portfolio value × (1 + Rate of return)] + Annual investment = Portfolio value a year later

The following is an example of the beginning of a wealth-building table, starting with the following assumptions:

* Begin at the end of the first year, assuming a year of investment contributions in your brokerage account.

* You contribute $500 per month.

* Your investments grow at 8% a year.

  Year 1 : $6,000

  Year 2 : $6,000 × (1.08) + $6,000 = $12,480

  Year 3 : $12,480 × (1.08) + $6,000 = $19,478

Build that formula into a spreadsheet and you can see how long it will take to reach your goal. Alternatively, if you know when you need to reach that goal, try different rates of return to determine the kind of returns needed to get you there at the proper time.

Before you move on to the last step, make sure you've avoided these four pitfalls:

- **Unreasonable expectations.** If your required rate of return is more than 10%, change your assumptions. Even 10% returns will be very, *very* difficult, and any plan based on the chance that you can earn more than 10% will fail more often than it succeeds. Don't kid yourself. Remember the 50-year-old from Chapter 1 with a $40,000 salary, no savings, lots of college expenses, and plans to retire a millionaire at 65? He failed before he started. Don't join him.

- **Forgetting inflation.** Over the last 80-plus years, inflation has averaged 3% annually. Make sure your spending estimates reflect inflation.

- **Forgetting expenses.** Try to add a few extra costs into your plan. You might get sick. Your house might burn down. Your brother-in-law might guilt-trip you into backing his restaurant, even though you know most restaurants fail. Life happens, and things that cost money are a part of life.

- **Underestimating your needs and life span.** If you think you'll need $60,000 a year, plan for $70,000. If you think you'll live 20 years past retirement, plan for 25. The more conservative your estimates, the more likely your investment plan will achieve its goals.

Making the Decision

OK, now you have an idea of what you want and the kind of returns that are required to get you there. That leaves just one question: What goes into the portfolio?

At this point, return to the rule of thumb that you should subtract your age from 110 and hold that percentage in stocks, and then build from there:

- Are you already wealthy? If so, add 5% to 10% to the stock allocation, depending on how comfortable you are with your level of wealth.
- How's your risk tolerance? Add or subtract up to 10% from the stock allocation depending on your tolerance for risk. Risk takers add to the allocation, risk avoiders subtract.
- When do you need the money? If your time horizon is more than 15 years, add up to 10% to the stock allocation. If you plan to use the money in less than 10 years, subtract up to 10%.

Now, armed with your revised stock and bond allocations, you must make one last leap—the leap from theory to practice. Projecting investment returns befuddles even the smartest, most detail-conscious analysts. Except in rare circumstances, you just can't predict the movements of the market. Going forward, our best estimate for long-term investment returns lies in the past.

While previous examples have used average returns for clarity, here you must rely on annualized returns. And over the long haul, large-company stocks have managed annualized returns of about 10%, long-term government bonds just over 6%, and Treasury bills about 3.5%.

Why Use Annualized Returns?

Annualized returns assume steady growth with no variations, and they will always lag the average annual return. In real life, investment returns vary from year to year, and the greater the variance, the greater the difference between average and annualized returns. For example:

- **The perfect world.** Invest $100 at exactly 10% this year and next year, and you'll have $121 at the end of two years. That's a two-year annualized return of 10%, and an average return of 10%.

- **Messy reality.** Invest $100 at a negative 20% this year and a positive 51% next year, and you'll have $121. That's a two-year annualized return of 10%, but an average return of more than 15%. A return of negative 35% for the first year and a positive 86% for the second year also gets you to $121, but with an average annual return of more than 25%.

Annualized returns tell a truer story. Since estimating the variance in annual returns over long periods is simply impossible, most long-term forecasts assume annualized returns.

While it takes a lot of work to calculate annualized portfolio returns, those three historical returns allow you to approximate the annual returns you can earn using large-company stocks, long-term government bonds, and short-term government bonds. Suppose your target allocation is 70% stocks and 30% bonds. The target annualized return of your portfolio is then 8.8%. Here's how to get there:

Equation

(Stock allocation × Stock returns) + (Bond allocation × Bond return)

(70% × 10%) + (30% × 6%) = 7.0% + 1.8% = 8.8%.

Remember, this is just an approximate portfolio return based on estimated stock and bond returns. It's definitely a work in progress—and at best a rough estimate—but now you have enough to compare your required return (the return you need to get where you wish to go) and your target return (the return implied by your target allocation). If your requirements exceed your target, you'll either have to take on more risk—as in choosing a higher stock allocation—or scale back on your investment targets.

Nobody likes to cut back on their goals or realize they can't live it up during retirement. When it comes to whether or not you can keep your house or cover your medical expenses after retirement, surprises can hurt. It's better to take the time to learn how far your resources can take you. Then you can adjust your goals to match your reality.

If your target exceeds your requirements, then life is good. You can reduce your risk to boost your chance of achieving your goals, or you can attempt to build extra wealth—potentially providing increased flexibility in the future.

Closing It Out

Whew. It took some work, but by now you should have a good idea about how to reach your financial destination without running out of money. After you master the concepts in this book, take the initiative to expand your knowledge of investing. Read books about investment analysis or delve deeper into the world of portfolio management—the list of suggested readings at the end of this book is a great place to start. It's never too late to begin working toward your goals for the future, and no matter how much you learn, you'll never figure everything out.

The journey never really ends. Fortunately, the strategies in this book should get you off to a good start.

SUGGESTIONS FOR FURTHER READING

Beating the Street
By Peter Lynch, 1993

Common Sense on Mutual Funds: 10th Anniversary Edition
By John Bogle, 2010

The Essays of Warren Buffett: Lessons for Corporate America, 3rd Edition
By Warren Buffett and Lawrence Cunningham, 2013

The Intelligent Investor: The Definitive Book on Value Investing
By Benjamin Graham, Jason Zweig, and Warren Buffett, 2006

The Armchair Economist: Economics and Everyday Life
By Steven Landsburg, 1995

Eight Steps to Seven Figures
By Charles Carlson, 2000

GLOSSARY OF TERMS

401(k) plan – A tax-preferred retirement plan offered to individuals by their employers, often with an element of employer matching.

Accounts receivable – Money owed to a company by customers in exchange for goods and services that have already been delivered. Also called receivables. Accounts receivables are recorded on the balance sheet as assets.

American depositary receipt (ADR) – A security that equates to a specified number of shares of a foreign company. Companies create ADRs to improve their visibility on U.S. exchanges. ADRs allow U.S. investors to more easily purchase stakes in foreign companies, as well as collect any dividends in U.S. currency.

Asset class – A type of asset, such as stocks or bonds. In some cases, investors will want to break a group into more specific classes, such as large-capitalization stocks and small-capitalization stocks.

Balance sheet – Presentation of a company's financial position. Key statistics presented include assets, debt, and equity.

Bear market – A period when securities prices are falling. Related terms include "bear"—the label for someone pessimistic about the market—and "bearish." See "Bull market."

Broker – An intermediary who buys or sells shares on behalf of investors. Full-service brokers provide personalized advice and other services to investors, in addition to handling transactions. Discount brokers make trades for investors but do not give advice. Not surprisingly, discount brokers charge lower commissions than full-service brokers.

Bull market – A period when securities prices are rising. Some investment philosophies set more specific parameters for a bull market, such as prices rising by a certain percentage or over a certain time. While investment professionals most often use the phrase in connection with stocks, it can apply to just about any financial market. Related terms include "bull"—the name for an investor optimistic about the market—and "bullish." See "Bear market."

Capital gain or loss – The profit or loss on the sale of an investment.

Commission – The fee a broker charges for buying or selling an investment.

Consensus estimate – The average estimate of Wall Street analysts who create financial projections for a given company, index, or commodity. Analysts provide targets for many statistics, but profit estimates are the easiest to find and the most frequently cited. See "Profit estimate."

Correction – A market movement that retraces all or part of an earlier movement. All markets correct. Bull markets correct downward and bear markets correct upward. Sometimes the correction transforms into a true change in direction, and sometimes stocks recover from the correction and return to their original path. Even the experts can't do much more than guess how a correction will turn out.

Correlation – A measure of how closely two investments move together.

Coupon – The interest rate on a bond at the time it's issued. Can also refer to the bond's semiannual payment.

Cyclical – Relating to a company or sector with operating results likely to vary based on economic or business conditions.

Derivative – One of many types of securities with prices derived from another asset. Stock options are among the most common stock derivatives. Because options provide the owner with the right to buy or sell shares at a preset price, the option price will rise and fall based on fluctuations in the price of the underlying stock. Some derivatives help investors hedge against risks, but others allow owners to reap gains (or losses) depending on changes in the value of the underlying asset.

Dividend – Periodic payment made by a company to its shareholders. Most U.S. companies that pay dividends distribute them quarterly. While most dividends are paid in cash, some companies prefer to issue new shares of stock.

Dividend reinvestment plan (DRIP) – A plan that allow investors to reinvest their dividends in company shares, and in many cases purchase additional shares directly from the company without using a broker.

Dow Jones Industrial Average – A price-weighted basket of 30 stocks often used as a proxy for the broader market. Common nicknames include "the Dow" and "the Industrials." Charles Dow, one of the founders of the *Wall Street Journal,* created the Dow Jones Industrial Average in 1896 as a tool for assessing market and economic trends. Often criticized for its price weighting (higher-priced stocks exert the most influence) and limited number of stocks, the Industrials remain the most commonly cited market proxy. When a pundit says "The market fell today," he's probably referring to the Dow Jones Industrial Average. See "S&P 500 Index."

Earnings release – A document that presents quarterly operating results, including sales and earnings. Many companies also release data from the balance sheet or statement of cash flows at this time. Most earnings releases contain both text and tables to explain how the company performed in the quarter. The release for the last quarter of the year will also address results for the entire year.

Face value – The original dollar amount borrowed by a bond issuer, also known as par value.

Fiscal quarter – A three-month period that makes up one-fourth of a company's fiscal year.

Fiscal year – A 12-month period used by a company to prepare financial statements. While most firms' fiscal years end in December, a company can set up its accounting to end the fiscal year whenever it wishes.

Fundamental analysis – Researching stocks based on operating statistics (growth rates, profit margins, debt levels, etc.), valuation, and other factors related to the company's business and market position.

Income statement – Presentation of a company's operating results. Key statistics presented include sales, profits, and number of shares outstanding.

Individual retirement account (IRA) – An investment account that allows individuals to grow their portfolio without paying taxes until the funds are withdrawn.

Inventory – Finished goods, goods partially completed, and raw materials slated for use in producing goods. Inventory is recorded as an asset on the balance sheet.

Invested capital – The sum of common equity, long-term debt, preferred stock, and minority interest. Analysts calculate invested capital as a proxy for the amount invested in the company by all stakeholders, assuming the company can tap into that capital for its own purposes.

Leverage – The amount of debt a company carries. In a more general sense, leverage represents the use of debt or other financial tools to boost returns, generally increasing risk at the same time.

Limit order – Instructions to a broker to buy or sell a stock at a specified price or better within a specified length of time. If the stock doesn't hit the target price before the deadline, the order expires without the broker making the trade.

Noncyclical – Relating to a company or sector with operating results that tend to remain steady regardless of economic or business conditions.

Par value – The original dollar amount borrowed by a bond issuer, also known as face value.

Penny stock – A term for low-priced stocks. Some investors use the term only for stocks trading below $1 per share, while others might consider anything below $5 a penny stock. While a few large companies trade at unusually low share prices, penny stocks are generally considered highly speculative and risky.

Portfolio – A general term for an investor's collection of securities.

Profit estimate – A projection of a company's future earnings. Wall Street analysts create financial models to forecast future results. The average of analyst estimates for a given period is called the consensus. See "Consensus estimate."

Quantitative analysis – Researching stocks based on financial models. Quantitative analysts rely on formulas that consider a variety of statistics and identify stocks that look attractive based on their models. In the industry, such models are often called "black boxes."

Return – The gain or loss on an investment. For the most part, returns consist of two components, capital gains or losses and income. Capital gains or losses reflect changes in the value of the investment. Most bonds and many stocks pay dividend or interest payments that provide income. Suppose you purchase a stock for $100 per share at the start of the year. At the end of the year, the shares have risen to $105. And along the way, the stock paid dividends of $1 per share. You earned a 6% return on the $100 investment, $5 in capital gains and $1 in income.

Risk aversion – Risk aversion is the reluctance of a person to make an investment with a highly uncertain payoff rather than another investment with a more certain, though often lower, return.

Risk tolerance – The level of volatility an investor can handle. This varies depending on risk aversion and level of wealth.

Roth IRA – An investment account that allows individuals to grow their portfolio tax-free, assuming certain requirements are met.

S&P 500 Index – A capitalization-weighted basket of 500 stocks designed to reflect the movement of the broader stock market, and particularly large-cap stocks. The index's creator, Standard & Poor's, estimates that the S&P 500 captures about 80% of U.S. stocks' total market capitalization. While most industry professionals regard the S&P 500 as a better market proxy than the Dow Jones Industrial Average, the Dow still retains its cachet with the media and generally gets top billing in financial newscasts. See "Dow Jones Industrial Average."

Securities – Financial instruments, mostly those that represent either an ownership interest (stocks) or a creditor interest (bonds). This general term can also refer to derivatives and other types of investments. See "Derivative."

Securities and Exchange Commission (SEC) – The U.S. government agency that regulates securities markets. Publicly traded companies must submit their quarterly and annual operating results to the SEC. These SEC filings typically contain far more information than the earnings release.

Short sale – A transaction in which an investor borrows stock and sells it, hoping to buy the shares back later at a lower price. Short selling is among the most common strategies investors use to profit from a hoped-for decline in a stock's price. Of course, if the share price rises, the investor may have to buy the shares back at a price higher than the original sale price.

Standard deviation – The range of returns around the average. Standard deviation measures volatility; the wider an investment's range of returns, the greater its risk. Suppose one stock rose 6% last year, 5% the year before, and 4% the year before that, for an average annual return of 5% and a standard deviation of 1%. Another stock fell 15% last year, gained 30% the year before, and was flat the year before that. The second stock also averaged an annual return of 5% but had a standard deviation of 23%, taking a riskier and more stomach-churning path.

Statement of cash flows – Presentation of a company's cash flows, broken up into three sections: operations, finance, and investment.

Stock split – The division of a share of stock into multiple, lower-priced shares. If XYZ Company trades for $100 per share and splits its stock 2-for-1, investors will receive two $50 shares for each $100 share. The split has no real economic impact, as it doesn't change the value of the investor's holdings. But in general, markets tend to perceive stock splits as positive. In some cases, companies do reverse splits, exchanging several inexpensive shares for one higher-priced share. Markets generally react negatively to reverse splits.

Stop-limit order – Instructions to a broker to buy or sell a stock at a set price, but only after a separate price threshold is reached. This order combines a stop order and a limit order.

Stop order – Instructions to a broker to buy or sell a security after its price passes a certain level. Once the price passes the threshold, the order converts to a market order, and the broker will make the trade at the best available price.

Technical analysis – Researching stocks based on market action. Technical analysts consider a stock's past price fluctuations— sometimes gauging movements of other stocks or indexes as well—to draw conclusions about whether the stock will rise or fall.

Ticker symbol – The letters used to identify a stock. Every stock has a ticker. For instance, Google trades under GOOG, Wal-Mart Stores under WMT, and AT&T under T.

Wall Street – The street in New York where a group of 24 stockbrokers gathered in 1792 to forge an agreement that blossomed into the first stock exchange in the United States. While Wall Street remains the geographic hub of the U.S. financial markets, it is also used as a general term for the investment community.

Yield – A stock's dividend as a percentage of the share price, or a bond's interest payment as a percentage of its price.

BIBLIOGRAPHY

Dow Jones Indexes. *Dow Jones Industrial Average.* December 31, 2011.
http://www.djindexes.com/mdsidx/downloads/brochure_info
/Dow_Jones_Industrial_Average_Brochure.pdf.

Fidelity. "A taxpayer's guide to 2013." *Fidelity Viewpoints.* February 27, 2013.
https://www.fidelity.com/viewpoints/personal-finance/taxpayers
-guide.

Internal Revenue Service. "Retirement topics – IRA contribution limits."
October 31, 2013.
http://www.irs.gov/Retirement-Plans/Plan-Participant,-Employee
/Retirement-Topics-IRA-Contribution-Limits.

Investment Company Institute. *Investment Company Fact Book.* Accessed
November 20, 2013.
http://www.ici.org/research/industry_research/fact_book.

Mintel Comperemedia. "The majority of investors still not familiar with
exchange traded funds (ETFs), reports Mintel." December 27, 2010.
http://www.comperemedia.com/press_releases/?__cc=1&doc_id=1103.

Morningstar, *Ibbotson SBBI 2013 Classic Yearbook.* 2013.
https://corporate.morningstar.com/ib/documents/MarketingOneSheets
/DataPublication/Class_ToC.pdf.

NASDAQ OMX. "What is NASDAQ?" Accessed November 20, 2013.
http://www.nasdaqomx.com/aboutus/company-information
/whatisnasdaq.

NYSE Euronext. "New York Stock Exchange." Accessed November 20, 2013.
https://www.nyx.com/en/who-we-are/history/new-york.

U.S. Securities and Exchange Commission. "Form 13F-reports filed by
institutional investment managers."
http://www.sec.gov/answers/form13f.htm.

U.S. Securities and Exchange Commission. *Invest Wisely: An Introduction
to Mutual Funds.*
http://www.sec.gov/investor/pubs/inwsmf.htm.

INDEX

Note: Pages number followed by "f" indicate figures; "t" tables.

15638456R00087

Made in the USA
San Bernardino, CA
02 October 2014